TANKMASTER

An essential guide to choosing you

MARINE

TROPICAL FISH

DICK MILLS

 INTERPET PUBLISHING

Author

Dick Mills, author of many aquarium books, is a former editor of The Aquarist & Pondkeeper magazine and also a Vice-President of the Federation of British Aquatic Societies. He has kept aquarium and pond fish continuously for the last 40 years, but also finds time to travel, when – as if by accident – he always manages to come across a public aquarium or two.

© 2001 Interpet Publishing,
Vincent Lane, Dorking, Surrey, RH4 3YX, England.
All rights reserved.
ISBN: 978-1-903098-04-2
This reprint 2009

Credits

Created and designed: Ideas into Print,
New Ash Green, Kent DA3 8JD, England.
Production management: Consortium, Poslingford,
Suffolk CO10 8RA, England.
Print production: Sino Publishing House Ltd., Hong Kong.
Printed and bound in Indonesia.

Below: The vivid colours of the purple firefish (Nemateleotris decora) *make this a popular fish for the marine aquarium. Although often referred to as a 'goby', it spends more time in midwater areas than its bottom-dwelling namesakes.*

Contents

Marine fishes live in extremely stable water conditions and have little or no tolerance towards any fluctuations. It is therefore essential that they are always kept in water of the highest quality; that is the real secret of successful marine fishkeeping.

Thanks to modern air freight services, the proportion of live, healthy fish arriving at their destination is much higher than it once was. As a result, availability is good and prices are relatively lower than they used to be. Today, increasing numbers of marine fish are being raised commercially in fish farms, rather than being wild-caught. In general, successful captive breeding has been limited to the smaller species.

In recent years, the trend has been away from keeping the more exotic – and endangered – species towards those that can be sustained successfully in captivity. Similarly, using synthetic coral as aquarium decoration is also contributing to the conservation of true underwater natural life, rather than over-collecting – and thus depleting – living specimens.

Keeping the fish happy

Mixing high-quality commercial 'salt mixes' with fresh water in the correct ratio to produce the required specific gravity (normally 1.022 at 25°C/77°F) is all that is needed to make marine aquarium water, but water quality will gradually decline, as indicated by a falling pH value (from an ideal of 8.3). To maintain good-quality water, install an efficient filtration system and carry out regular partial water changes – usually about 25% every three to four weeks.

Feeding

A major problem associated with keeping wild-caught fish in captivity is providing them with their natural diet. Certain marine fish have very specific dietary requirements that have not been totally replicated by fish food manufacturers, and many unfortunate fishes gradually starve to death. However, for the most part, your local aquatic store will have a wide range of frozen foods specially

Left: Prepare the initial volume of synthetic seawater in the aquarium itself. The heating system provides the correct temperature, and water movement from the aeration or filtration system ensures the salt is rapidly mixed. Prepare smaller amounts in a bucket for partial water changes.

Below: Check the specific gravity with a hydrometer. The water surface meniscus should be level with the desired value, here 1.022. Add more salt mix or water as needed.

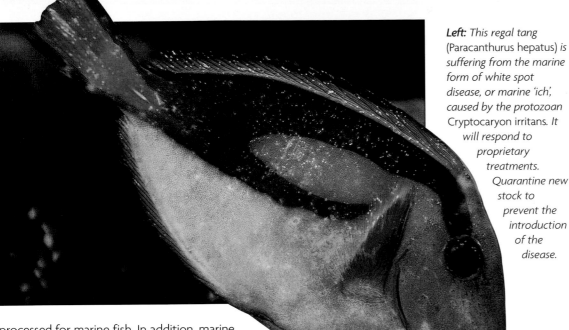

processed for marine fish. In addition, marine fish will accept flake food and many appreciate vegetable matter, such as scalded lettuce leaves. Any uneaten food soon decomposes and pollutes the aquarium. Only provide enough food for the fish to consume within a few minutes at any one time.

Health care

Most ailments in the aquarium are stress-related. Many of the easily detected common ailments can be treated successfully using commercially available treatments. When attempting to diagnose illnesses, always check the aquarium conditions – especially water parameters – first. Attention to aquarium hygiene, modest stocking levels and quarantining all new stock will do much to ensure that your aquarium remains stress- and disease-free.

Just fish?

Keeping fish and invertebrates together in the same aquarium is a little too advanced for you if you are a novice marine fishkeeper. Without some experience, you may choose fish that coincidentally in nature include invertebrates in their daily diet! This guide will limit its considerations to choosing marine fishes for a fish-only collection.

Compatibility

The only constraint we must exercise over the choice of fish is that of extremes of size and sociability. Obviously, very large fishes cannot co-exist with very small ones and, sad to say, not every fish is tolerant of its own species or of other fish that are the same shape or colour as itself.

The numbers game

The 'fishkeeping data' included on the following pages assumes that your marine fish will be housed in a tank measuring 90cm long by 38cm high by 30cm front to back (36x15x12in). Applying the guide of 120cm^2 of water surface per centimetre of fish body length (excluding the tail), this tank's eventual total fish-holding capacity will be about 23cm of 'fish'. (This is equivalent to 1in of fish length per 48in^2 of tank surface area.) Do not add all the fish to the tank at once; build up to this total progressively over several months to enable the filtration system to cope with the increasing bioload.

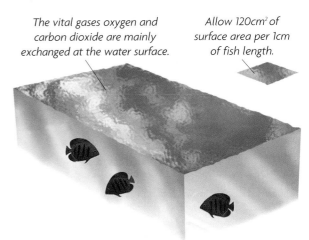

The vital gases oxygen and carbon dioxide are mainly exchanged at the water surface.

Allow 120cm^2 of surface area per 1cm of fish length.

***Above:** The maximum fish-holding capacity of any aquarium is governed by its water surface area. Total volume of water in the tank is irrelevant in this respect.*

Anemonefishes & damselfishes

The family Pomacentridae contains two groups of fishes kept by most marine fishkeepers as initial stock fish when first setting up the marine aquarium. The reasons for this are easy to understand; the fish are hardy, inexpensive and readily available. Because of their hardiness, they can tolerate early introduction into a newly set up aquarium that may not be sufficiently established to support more delicate species. However, this is no excuse for the impatient fishkeeper to skimp on preparing the aquarium properly before introducing any fish.

The family consists of two distinct groups of fishes, both of which need to feel secure within the aquarium. Anemonefishes, as their name implies, seek refuge within the tentacles of a sea anemone, while damselfishes tend to congregate around the branches of any stands of coral. Each group has an individual swimming style: anemonefishes waddle about, while damselfishes tend to have a more vertical bobbing action.

Caring for these fish is straightforward. They will accept most foods and are not too antagonistic towards other fishes in the aquarium. Damselfishes may squabble amongst themselves, so provide an aquarium large enough to give each fish a reasonable amount of territory. Several species are likely to breed within the confines of the aquarium, depositing and guarding their eggs in much the same way as freshwater cichlids.

Above: *This spinecheek anemonefish (Premnas biaculeatus) is the largest of the anemonefishes, but still seeks the reassurance of safety amongst the tentacles of a sea anemone.*

FAMILY: POMACENTRIDAE (ANEMONEFISHES)

This clownfish, also known as the tomato clown or fire clown, is slightly larger than the common clown (page 10) and lacks the vertical white banding found on some species. Its red-orange body is merely marked by an oval, dark brown patch two thirds along the flank. All the fins are plain red-orange in colour. It has been reported that juveniles have a vertical thin white line passing down over their head, just behind the eye, but this fades with maturity.

Compatibility

While happy to be associated with the sea anemone, this species is a bold feeder and at times may become aggressive towards any other fish entering its territory.

▶ Origins

The Andaman and Nicobar Islands, Malaysia and Java.

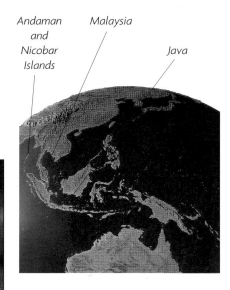

Andaman and Nicobar Islands   Malaysia   Java

Ungainly swimmers

The name 'clownfish' has been applied to these fishes because of their waddling swimming action. In some literature they may even be called clown anemonefish.

The composition of the mucus covering the skin prevents the stinging cells (nematocysts) of the sea anemone's tentacles from 'firing', thus providing the fish with immunity.

▶ *Fishkeeping data*

Number per aquarium: Two to three, plus a suitable sea anemone.
Community/species tank: Community.
Swimming area: Middle and lower levels.
Food: All prepared foods, including freeze-dried and frozen, plus some vegetable matter.
Compatibility: Peaceful.
Availability: Regularly available (wild-caught).
Captive breeding: No information.

COMMON CLOWNFISH • *Amphiprion percula*

FAMILY: POMACENTRIDAE (ANEMONEFISHES)

For most people, the definitive anemonefish is the common clown. It is able to live within the tentacles of the sea anemone with impunity, because the mucus on its skin prevents the sea anemone's stinging cells from operating. The ability to dash into the tentacles when pursued by predators stands the clownfish in good stead, as its pursuers will not be similarly immune. Some authors are of the opinion that as a reward for acting as a safe haven, the sea anemone benefits from particles of food accidentally (or perhaps purposely?) dropped by the returning clownfish. Although this mutual friendship may be classed by some as symbiosis, neither of the animals is strictly dependent on the other and perhaps the more correct term for this association would be commensalism.

Fishkeeping data

Number per aquarium: Two to three, plus a suitable sea anemone.
Community/species tank: Community.
Swimming area: Middle and lower levels.
Food: All prepared foods, including freeze-dried and frozen, plus some vegetable matter.
Compatibility: Peaceful.
Availability: Regularly available (tank-bred and wild-caught).
Captive breeding: Possible.

Papua New Guinea

Solomon Islands

Great Barrier Reef

Origins

One of the most widespread species in the genus, ranging from Papua New Guinea to the Solomon Islands and Australia's Great Barrier Reef.

The distinctive body pattern is shared by the almost identical species, A. ocellaris, the false clown anemonefish. However, it is easy to distinguish between them, because the common clownfish has the wider black markings.

Breeding

Eggs are deposited and fertilised on a firm surface such as a nearby rock. The parents guard them until the fry hatch. Clownfishes are often increasingly available from captive-bred stocks, thus lessening the need for wild-caught specimens.

10

PINK SKUNK CLOWNFISH ● *Amphiprion perideraion*

FAMILY: POMACENTRIDAE (ANEMONEFISHES)

As its popular name suggests, the body colour of this clownfish is more subtle than the garish hues of the preceding species. A thin, vertical white stripe crosses the body at the rear of the gill cover and another white line runs from the top of the head right along the top of the dorsal ridge to the caudal peduncle. The pectoral, pelvic and anal fins are the same colour as the body, but the dorsal and caudal fins are almost colourless, with just a tinge of yellow. The skunk anemonefish, *Amphiprion akallopisos*, is similarly coloured, but lacks the white vertical stripe on the head.

Over its natural distribution range, it is usually found within the tentacles of the sea anemone *Heteractis magnifica*.

Sex reversal

The genus is also noted for its sex reversal characteristics. However, in this instance, all fish mature as males, only changing into a dominant female in order to head small colonies.

Thailand   Japan

▶ Origins

From Thailand to Samoa, including waters south of Japan down as far as the Great Barrier Reef and New Caledonia.

Samoa

New Caledonia

▶ *Fishkeeping data*

Number per aquarium: Two to three, plus a suitable sea anemone.
Community/species tank: Community.
Swimming area: Middle and lower levels.
Food: All prepared foods, including freeze-dried and frozen, plus some vegetable matter.
Compatibility: Peaceful.
Availability: Less frequently available (wild-caught).
Captive breeding: No information.

FAMILY: POMACENTRIDAE (ANEMONEFISHES)

This is one of the largest clownfish. In addition to this identifying factor, it also has two rearward-facing sharp spines on each cheek just below the eye. This feature accounts for its alternative common name of spinecheek anemonefish. The orange and red body colour is more intense in the male fish and is crossed vertically by three narrow white bands. The female fish is much more likely to attain the maximum size and her body colour can be much darker, almost black, with less distinct bands. These may almost disappear in some specimens.

Like all wild-caught anemonefishes, the maroon clownfish is susceptible to stress arising from poor handling and poor aquarium conditions. However, specimens obtained commercially from captive breeding programmes are said to be much hardier.

It is usually found exclusively with the bubbletop sea anemone, *Entacmaea quadricolor*, although in the aquarium it may not be quite so dependent on a sea anemone as its relatives.

▶ Origins

Western Indonesia as far north as Taiwan and south to the northern end of the Great Barrier Reef.

Taiwan

Western Indonesia

Great Barrier Reef

▶ *Fishkeeping data*

Number per aquarium: One.
Community/species tank: Community.
Swimming area: Middle and lower levels.
Food: All prepared foods, including freeze-dried and frozen, plus some vegetable matter.
Compatibility: May bully.
Availability: Frequently available (wild-caught).
Captive breeding: Possible.

Its larger size, deep orange-red coloration and three white stripes makes the maroon clownfish easy to identify.

SERGEANT MAJOR ● *Abudefduf saxatilis*

FAMILY: POMACENTRIDAE (DAMSELFISHES)

Look out from a glass-bottomed boat anywhere in the tropics and you are bound to see an oval, silvery fish with a number of vertical dark bands across its sides. In military terms, the sergeant major has an enormous parade ground, being found on rocky shores and coral reefs in both the Atlantic and Indo-Pacific areas, although to be accurate, there is more than one species with this common name. For example, *A. saxatilis* is from the Atlantic, while *A. vaigiensis* is found from the Red Sea eastwards to Lord Howe Island in the Pacific, but *A. abdominalis* is restricted to the Hawaiian islands.

The body coloration is similar (give or take a blotch or two) from species to species. The body shape is very reminiscent of the freshwater sunfish, although the caudal peduncle is much shorter. Sergeant majors can be territorially aggressive.

Fishkeeping data

Number per aquarium: One.
Community/species tank: Community.
Swimming area: Middle and upper levels.
Food: All foods.
Compatibility: May bully.
Availability: Usually available (wild-caught).
Captive breeding: No information.

Pacific Ocean

> **Origins**

The Atlantic and Indo-Pacific areas.

Indian Ocean

Atlantic Ocean

Spacious aquariums can contain more fish from one species, providing they each have ample 'territorial space'.

FAMILY: POMACENTRIDAE (DAMSELFISHES)

With the demoiselles we enter a veritable minefield of identification problems, because there are so many similar-looking, brilliantly blue-coloured species from several different genera – without counting the blue-only juvenile forms. *C. parasema* has a touch more yellow to its posterior end than most, which should make identification slightly less problematical.

All damselfish are territorial and on the aggressive side. They will quarrel if there is not enough room (or too few hideaways) in the aquarium. Introducing lone specimens (often of any species of fish, not just the same species) into an aquarium already inhabited by damsels is asking for trouble. The best way to encourage them to settle in is to introduce a small number at once. Another trick is to relocate the aquarium decorations just before making any new introduction, so that everyone is too busy choosing new territories to pick a fight.

Electric blue, although a strikingly dazzling colour, is common amongst several similar species of damselfishes.

Ryuku Islands

Philippines

Sulawesi

Papua New Guinea

Solomon Islands

▶ Origins

Philippines, Sulawesi, New Guinea, Solomon Islands and Ryuku Islands.

The amount of yellow on an otherwise blue fish may help with a more positive identification of these fishes.

▶ *Fishkeeping data*

Number per aquarium: Two or three (or maybe two or three single specimens from different genera).
Community/species tank: Community.
Swimming area: Middle and upper levels.
Food: All foods.
Compatibility: Territorial, pugnacious.
Availability: Often available (wild-caught).
Captive breeding: No information.

HUMBUG • *Dascyllus aruanus*

FAMILY: POMACENTRIDAE (DAMSELFISHES)

This fish's common name may intrigue anyone who is unfamiliar with the black-and-white striped peppermint confection of the same name.

The high-backed white body is crossed vertically by three black bands, which are united by a thick black edge along the top of the dorsal fin. The pelvic and anal fins are also black, but the pectoral and caudal fins remain clear. *Dascyllus melanurus* is often confused with this species. Although it lacks the black edge to the dorsal fin, it does have a black area across the caudal fin.

Damselfish congregate around coral heads and are only too quick to dash into the safety of the coral's branches. There is bound to be a wealth of such sanctuaries in this fish's natural range, from the Red Sea eastwards to Lord Howe Island in the Pacific.

Fishkeeping data

Number per aquarium: Two to three (or maybe two to three single specimens from different genera).
Community/species tank: Community.
Swimming area: Middle and upper levels.
Food: All foods.
Compatibility: Peaceful.
Availability: Regularly available (wild-caught).
Captive breeding: No information.

Red Sea

Origins

From the Red Sea eastwards to Lord Howe Island in the Pacific.

Lord Howe Island

Domino, or three-spot damselfish

The three white spots on the jet black body of D. trimaculatus are very reminiscent of a domino piece. A white spot appears on each side of the body just below the dorsal fin, with a third spot located on the dorsal surface just above the forehead. This coloration is limited to the juvenile form, as the adult fish is a sooty-grey, with less distinct (if at all visible) white markings.

D. trimaculatus has a similar distribution to D. aruanus and the same requirements in captivity.

A feature of the juvenile fish's behaviour is its association with large sea anemones, a trait it loses when adult.

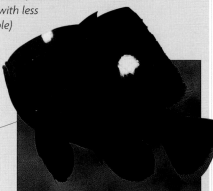

Angelfishes

The Family Pomacanthidae contains many brilliantly coloured fishes that range in size from very small to species that would feel more at home in a public aquarium. For example, members of the genus *Centropyge* can be accommodated quite easily in the home aquarium, whereas members of the genus *Pomacanthus* require much larger living quarters. A distinguishing physical feature of these fishes is the backward-projecting spine on the rear of the gill cover. Another characteristic of some members of this family is the complete difference in colour patterning between juvenile and adult specimens.

Many angelfish are specific feeders and, unfortunately, it may not always be possible to acclimatise them to aquarium life. In the wild, some restrict their diets to sponges and it is difficult to provide a continuous supply of their required food.

Spawning usually occurs in the early evening, when pairs of fishes come together to release free-floating eggs at the climax of their courtship manoeuvring. However, this is not likely to happen within the aquarium.

Above: *The queen angelfish,* Holacanthus ciliaris, *is one of the relatively few species of angelfish to grace the warm waters of the Caribbean.*

BICOLOR ANGELFISH ● *Centropyge bicolor*

FAMILY: POMACANTHIDAE (ANGELFISHES)

As can be deduced from its distribution range, this species is a common occurrence. Its very distinctive patterning – forward half and caudal fin bright yellow, the remainder royal blue – makes identification simple. The blue area on the forehead helps to distinguish it from the very similar Coco's pigmy angelfish, *C. joculator*, which has a more swept-back forward edge to the blue area of coloration and orange-edged dorsal and anal fins. As it often feels insecure, the bicolor angelfish prefers areas of rocky rubble that offer welcome boltholes.

▶ Origins

From Malaysia to Samoa, Japan to northwestern Australia.

Malaysia

Japan

Northwestern Australia

Samoa

The coloration of this fish is not dissimilar to that of the much larger rock beauty, Holacanthus tricolor, *which lacks the dark patch above the eye.*

Cherubfish

The elongated oval body of C. argi (8cm/3.2in) is a deep royal blue that extends into all the fins except the pectorals, which share the bright daffodil-yellow colour of the head. The cherubfish frequents rocky rubble around the coral reefs of Bermuda, Florida and the Caribbean. It feeds mostly on algal growths, so provide some vegetable matter within its diet.

▶ Fishkeeping data

Number per aquarium: One or an established pair.
Community/species tank: Community.
Swimming area: Middle and lower levels.
Food: Appreciates some vegetable matter.
Compatibility: Peaceful.
Availability: Frequently available (wild-caught).
Captive breeding: No information.

FAMILY: POMACANTHIDAE (ANGELFISHES)

The distinctive coloration of this species can lead to a little confusion between it and its relative, Herald's angelfish *(C. heraldi)*, but the latter lacks the outlining blue of the dorsal, anal and caudal fins and the blue lips. However, just to make things difficult, a local population around the Cocos-Keeling and Christmas Islands in the Indian Ocean does lack the blue outline. Add to this the fact that the juvenile form of the mimic surgeonfish, *Acanthurus pyroferus*, which shares it distribution area (which also reaches as far as Easter Island), is also a plain yellow colour, and you have even more opportunity for confusion.

Closer examination reveals that the lemonpeel hybridises with the pearlscale angelfish *(C. vroliki),* and Eibl's angelfish *(C. eibli).*

Right: *Look for the blue-edged fins if you are seeking this species, otherwise you might end up with something completely different, such as a juvenile surgeonfish.*

▶ Fishkeeping data

Number per aquarium: One or an established pair.
Community/species tank: Community.
Swimming area: Middle and lower levels.
Food: Appreciates some vegetable matter.
Compatibility: Peaceful.
Availability: Frequently available (wild-caught).
Captive breeding: No information.

▶ Origins

Cocos-Keeling and Christmas Islands; Ryukyu, Marianas to Rapa Island. Usually absent from Indo-Australian waters.

Ryukyu Islands

Marianas Islands

Christmas Island

Cocos-Keeling Islands

Rapa Island

FAMILY: POMACANTHIDAE (ANGELFISHES)

The coloration of the bright-orange body with its bright-yellow central area is further enhanced by vertical bands of deep blue-black. The edges of the soft-rayed portions of the dorsal and anal fins also have this blue-black coloration, but the caudal fin is red, shading to yellow. This species is somewhat shy and prefers to stay close to any convenient sanctuary-offering coral outcrop.

Male fish tend to be larger than females. All the fish start out as females, then males develop amongst a harem later.

▶ Origins

From Palau, just east of the Philippines, to Samoa and the Great Barrier Reef, although less frequent around Hawaii.

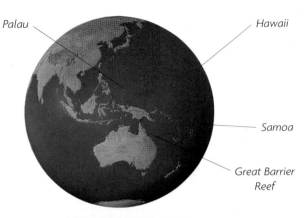

Palau

Hawaii

Samoa

Great Barrier Reef

With its red-orange coloration and contrasting purple-blue-black stripes, the resemblance to a flickering fire justifiably provides the popular name of flame angelfish.

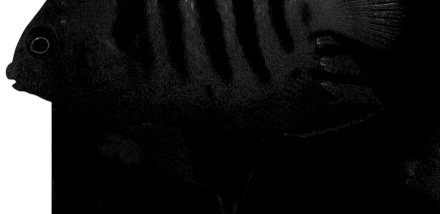

▶ *Fishkeeping data*

Number per aquarium: One or an established pair.
Community/species tank: Community.
Swimming area: Middle and lower levels.
Food: Appreciates some vegetable matter.
Compatibility: Peaceful.
Availability: Frequently available (wild-caught).
Captive breeding: No information.

EMPEROR ANGELFISH ● *Pomacanthus imperator*

Size: 40cm (16in)

FAMILY: POMACANTHIDAE (ANGELFISHES)

This fish is a favourite (and very recognisable) species with fishkeepers. The body is traversed with diagonal, alternating stripes of blue and yellow, the snout is grey, the eye is hidden within a blue-edged dark stripe and a yellow face mask is interrupted by a further dark area down across the gill cover. The anal fin is purple with red streaking, while the dorsal and caudal fins are yellow. It is reported that specimens from the Indian Ocean have rounded dorsal fins, not pointed as in other cases. However, all this gorgeous patterning is in the future because, like many of its relatives, the juvenile form is dark blue with white markings, in a vaguely concentric form in this particular species.

Juveniles tend to keep in or around boltholes and ledges in coral outcrops, but the adults are much bolder on the seaward coral faces of reefs that occur throughout its large distribution area.

Above: Like many juvenile angelfish, the young emperor angelfish does not resemble the adult coloration form in any way.

▶ Origins

From the Red Sea to Hawaii, Japan to south of Tahiti.

Japan

Hawaii

Red Sea

Tahiti

▶ Fishkeeping data

Number per aquarium: One.
Community/species tank: Community.
Swimming area: All levels.
Food: Appreciates some vegetable matter.
Compatibility: Peaceful.
Availability: Frequently available (wild-caught).
Captive breeding: No information.

As if any further decoration was necessary, the emperor angelfish's stunning patterning is supplemented by a bright yellow caudal fin.

FRENCH ANGELFISH ● *Pomacanthus paru*

FAMILY: POMACANTHIDAE (ANGELFISHES)

Most marine fishkeepers will be more familiar with the juvenile form of this species and its black body (and fins) crossed by vertical yellow stripes. This is a far more interesting pattern than the adult fish's rather drab grey-black ground colour with a faint dusting of yellowish flecks. Again, the adult fish is a rather large proposition to take on for the average domestic aquarium.

▸ Fishkeeping data

Number per aquarium: One.
Community/species tank: Community.
Swimming area: All levels.
Food: Appreciates some vegetable matter.
Compatibility: Peaceful.
Availability: Frequently available (wild-caught).
Captive breeding: Fry have been produced using the 'hand-stripping' method similar to that used for goldfish.

Left *The adult French angelfish is drab grey with some yellow speckles; this semi-adult still bears traces of the vertical yellow stripes seen in the juvenile form shown on the right.*

Gulf of Mexico

Brazil

Ascension Island

▸ Origins

A far-ranging species covering waters of the northern Gulf of Mexico to Brazil. There are even some reports of central Atlantic sightings around Ascension Island.

▸ Breeding

French angelfish tend to pair-bond in nature. The actual spawning process is a leisurely affair conducted in deeper water, with eggs being expelled and fertilised as the two fish swim upwards through the water. Reports indicate that breeding through 'hand-stripping' adult fish of eggs and sperm (in a similar fashion to goldfish) is possible.

Butterflyfishes

Members of the Family Chaetodontidae are not dissimilar in shape or coloration to the angelfishes, but lack the spine on the gill cover. Furthermore, feeding can present similar problems (see page 16). Most of the butterflyfishes have sharply pointed heads, often with elongated snouts that are ideal for picking among the coral for their food. They are typically active during daylight hours and retreat amongst the coral heads at night.

Although this group contains some of the most beautiful fishes to be seen around the coral reef, it is in their own best interests that they are left in their natural habitat. However, their expensive price tag will always mean that they are desired by the ambitious fishkeeper, who in all probability will be disappointed at their relatively short life in captivity, usually due to feeding problems. Because they are grazers of polyps and sponges, there is the added problem of keeping them in a reef tank containing live corals.

On the credit side, established pairs of butterflyfish generally do well, although their degree of 'hardiness' is often due to their method of capture — net-caught specimens being far hardier than those captured using drugs.

Above: *The Red Sea bannerfish,* Heniochus intermedius, *naturally occurs in shoals. It is important to take such sociable behaviour into account when choosing fish for the aquarium.*

FAMILY: CHAETODONTIDAE (BUTTERFLYFISHES)

Many species of *Chaetodon* within the same distribution range are similarly coloured and the threadfin butterflyfish shares its 'herring-bone' striped patterning of grey-black stripes on a silvery yellow background with two or three relatives. Additionally, the hiding of the eye in a vertical dark band is a common feature amongst butterflyfishes in general, serving to protect this vital organ from attack. It is especially effective when supplemented by a replica, or decoy, eye marking elsewhere on the body.

The common name refers to a threadlike extension to the rear of the yellow rear portion of the dorsal fin. While threadfins usually have an 'eyespot' in the dorsal fin's yellow area, some populations on the seaward side of reefs do not. Normal foods include polyps, anemones and algae.

Fishkeeping data

Number per aquarium: One.
Community/species tank: Community.
Swimming area: All levels.
Food: Polyps, anemones and algae, but will take prepared foods.
Compatibility: Peaceful.
Availability: Frequently available (wild-caught).
Captive breeding: No information.

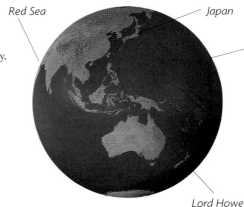

Red Sea   Japan

Hawaii

Origins

A wide-ranging distribution from the Red Sea to Hawaii, Japan to Lord Howe Island.

Lord Howe Island

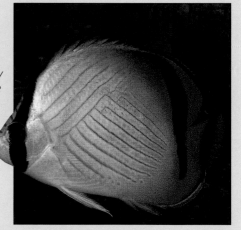

Vagabond butterflyfish

Chaetodon vagabundus *may be distinguished from the threadfin by the black border running around the rear edge of the body and around the rear edges of the dorsal and anal fins. Two vertical black bars appear on the yellow caudal fin. The forehead is less steeply inclined. The diet follows that for the threadfin and the distribution area is similar.*

COPPERBAND or BEAKED BUTTERFLYFISH ● *Chelmon rostratus*

FAMILY: CHAETODONTIDAE (BUTTERFLYFISHES)

While many butterflyfishes have almost identical coloration, the copperband is in a class of its own, except maybe for the very similar ocellate coralfish, *Parachaetodon ocellatus*, found further westwards. However, its body shape is more rhomboid, while the copperband's is oblong.

The silvery body is crossed vertically by five black-edged orange bands that reach into the yellow-and-blue-edged pelvic, anal and dorsal fins. There is a false eyespot in the rear portion of the dorsal fin. The main physical characteristic (apart from the coloration) is the long beaklike snout – ideal for reaching into coralline crevices for food.

The copperband may be slow to acclimatise to tank conditions and appears to do best in a well-established reef aquarium, where it can find enough to satisfy its coral-pecking instincts.

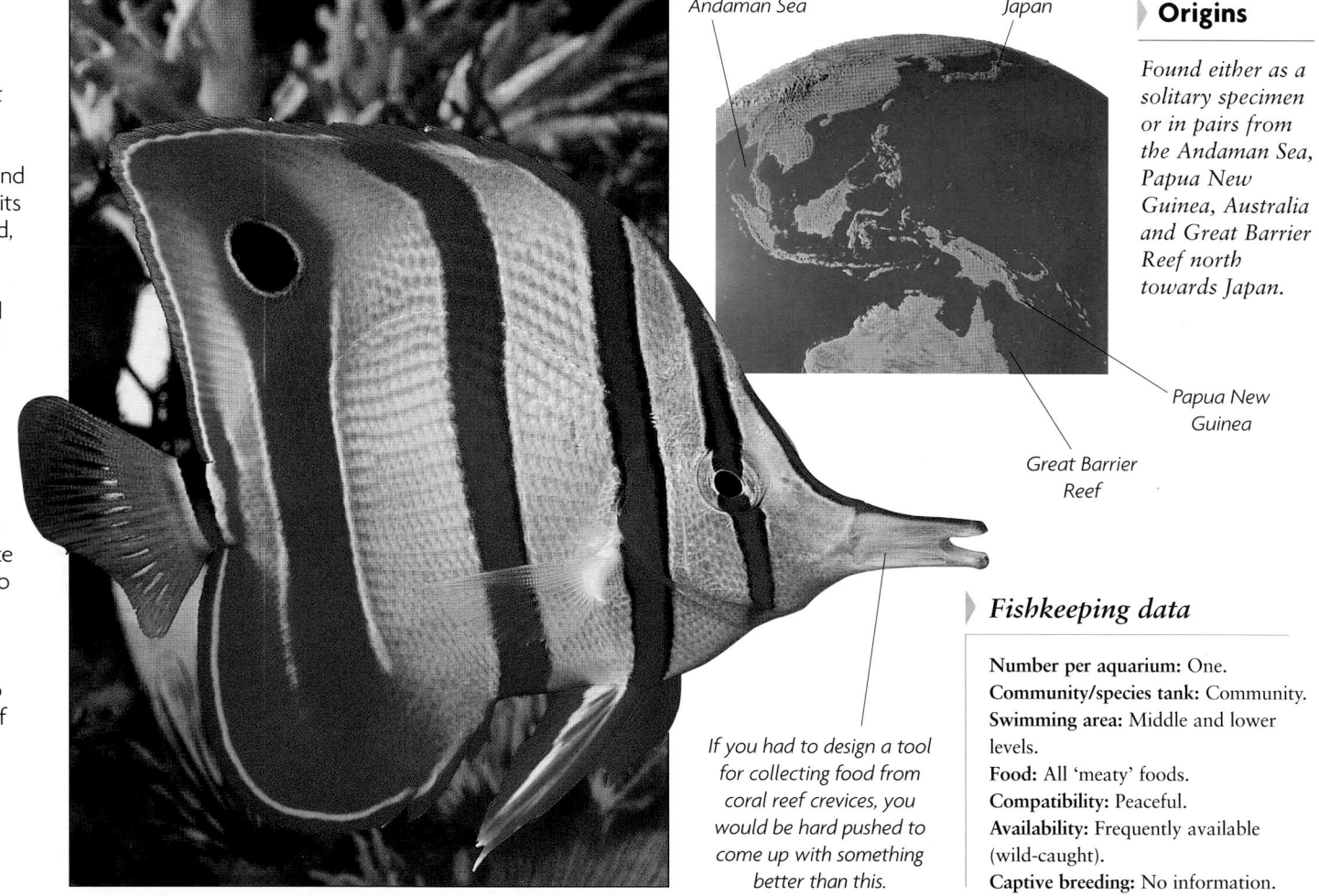

If you had to design a tool for collecting food from coral reef crevices, you would be hard pushed to come up with something better than this.

Andaman Sea

Japan

Papua New Guinea

Great Barrier Reef

► Origins

Found either as a solitary specimen or in pairs from the Andaman Sea, Papua New Guinea, Australia and Great Barrier Reef north towards Japan.

► Fishkeeping data

Number per aquarium: One.
Community/species tank: Community.
Swimming area: Middle and lower levels.
Food: All 'meaty' foods.
Compatibility: Peaceful.
Availability: Frequently available (wild-caught).
Captive breeding: No information.

LONGNOSED BUTTERFLYFISH ● *Forcipiger longirostris*

FAMILY: CHAETODONTIDAE (BUTTERFLYFISHES)

This species not only looks extremely similar to its relative, *F. flavissimus*, but also shares much of its distribution area. For those wishing to differentiate between the two species, *F. longirostris* has the longer snout and the steeper forehead, while *F. flavissimus* has a larger gape to its mouth.

The head coloration serves two purposes: the black upper half protects the eye (there is a small eyespot on the rear of the anal fin to divert attack away from the real eye), while the silver lower half effectively breaks up the fish profile, again perhaps to prevent detection from would-be predators. The whole body rearwards of the gills, together with the pelvic, dorsal and anal fins, is bright yellow, with bright blue on the edges of the single fins. The caudal fin is colourless.

This is another instance of disruptive coloration, with bold areas of different colour that break up the fish's outline.

Origins

From East Africa to Hawaii, Japan to the Austral Islands, including the Great Barrier Reef.

East Africa

Japan

Hawaii

Austral Islands

Great Barrier Reef

Note that the real eye is hidden in a dark area with a 'decoy' eye prominently displayed just below the caudal peduncle.

Longnoses make good aquarium subjects because, despite their specialised 'feeding equipment', they will accept a wide variety of foods.

Fishkeeping data

Number per aquarium: One.
Community/species tank: Community.
Swimming area: Middle and lower levels.
Food: All 'meaty' foods.
Compatibility: Peaceful.
Availability: Frequently available (wild-caught).
Captive breeding: No information.

Wrasses

The Family Labridae contains very many species of all shapes and sizes, although usually it is only juvenile members of the species that are suitable for the home aquarium. Again, there may be a vast difference both in colour and patterning between juvenile and adult forms.

All wrasses appear to rest at night, often burying themselves in the substrate or spinning a cocoon of mucus to form a 'sleeping bag'. An aquarium furnished with many nooks and crannies is ideal for wrasses.

Perhaps the best-known species is the cleaner wrasse, *Labroides dimidiatus*, which feeds off parasites on other fishes. Unfortunately, this habit pushes the species into a 'specific feeder' category, which means that in the average aquarium (containing few parasites) there may well not be enough food for this fish to thrive. For this reason – apart from this reference – it has been omitted from this guide.

Many wrasses are brilliantly coloured and would make attractive aquarium subjects. The larger species are not recommended for a reef-type tank, although smaller species are much more satisfactory in this respect.

Above: *The banana, or canary, wrasse (Halichoeres chrysus) is modestly sized, and a trio can be comfortably housed in the average-sized aquarium to form the basic, 'starting off' collection.*

CUBAN or SPOTFIN HOGFISH • *Bodianus pulchellus*

FAMILY: LABRIDAE (WRASSES)

The stocky but streamlined body is bright crimson-red for most of its length; only the top half of the caudal peduncle is bright yellow. The pelvic, dorsal and anal fins are also scarlet, while the caudal fin is mostly yellow; only the bottom edge carries the remainder of the red colour from the body. The clear pectoral fins feature a black blotch at their tips. In some specimens, a lateral white stripe may be present.

This bold species acts as a cleanerfish when young and is often found in close association with the bluehead wrasse, *Thalassoma bifasciatum*.

Right: The spotfin hogfish takes its name from the black blotch on the end of each pectoral fin.

Fishkeeping data

Number per aquarium: One.
Community/species tank: Community, but not with invertebrates.
Swimming area: Middle and lower levels.
Food: All 'meaty' foods.
Compatibility: Usually peaceful but intolerant of its own kind.
Availability: Frequently available (wild-caught).
Captive breeding: No information.

Origins

Wide-ranging across the Caribbean, from Florida to Brazil.

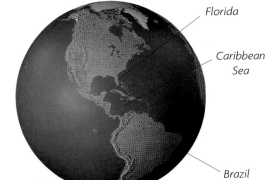

Florida

Caribbean Sea

Brazil

HARLEQUIN TUSKFISH ● *Choerodon (Lienardella) fasciatus*

FAMILY: LABRIDAE (WRASSES)

The coloration of this fish is quite stunning, with blue-edged bright orange bands crossing the blue-silver body vertically. The pelvic, dorsal and anal fins are also orange-red with blue edges. The body area around the caudal peduncle is dark blue and the caudal fin is white with a red final edge. The teeth are protrusible, ideal for moving rocks around in order to get at the invertebrate food beneath them, or for wrenching molluscs from rocks.

This adult tuskfish has lost the 'eyespots' seen on the dorsal, anal and pelvic fins of the juvenile form.

▶ Origins

Often found as solitary specimens in their native waters, ranging from Taiwan, Ryukyu Islands to Australia and the Great Barrier Reef.

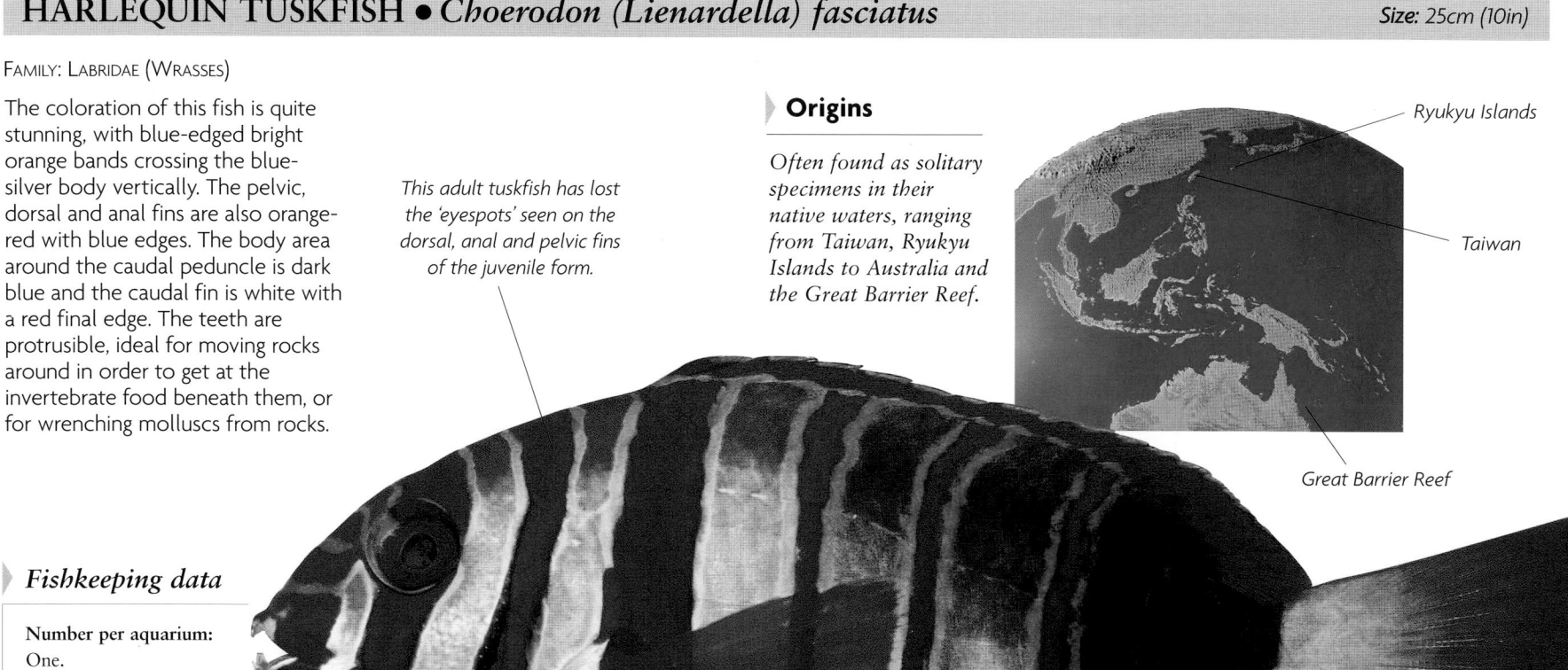

Ryukyu Islands

Taiwan

Great Barrier Reef

▶ *Fishkeeping data*

Number per aquarium: One.
Community/species tank: Community, but not with invertebrates.
Swimming area: Middle and lower levels.
Food: All 'meaty' foods.
Compatibility: Usually peaceful but intolerant of its own kind.
Availability: Frequently available (wild-caught).
Captive breeding: No information.

BIRDMOUTH or INDIAN OCEAN BIRD WRASSE ● *Gomphosus coeruleus*

Size: 28cm (11in)

FAMILY: LABRIDAE (WRASSES)

The birdmouth wrasse is aptly named, for not only does it have an extended snout reminiscent of a bird's beak, but also a curious swimming action that gives the impression that the fish is 'flying' through the water with a swooping action that is more avian than piscine.

The body of the male fish is green-blue, with a semicircle of yellow in the caudal fin. The dorsal and anal fins have yellow borders and the pectoral fins are black. The female is a dull brown colour.

This constantly active species does not burrow into the substrate at night, but hides up amongst the coral.

Given its long, beaklike snout and the flapping wing action of its pectoral fins, this fish's common name is particularly appropriate.

▶ Origins

A wide natural distribution, ranging from the Red Sea to Hawaii, Ryukyu Islands to Lord Howe Island.

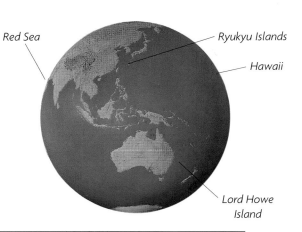

Red Sea

Ryukyu Islands

Hawaii

Lord Howe Island

▶ *Fishkeeping data*

Number per aquarium: One.
Community/species tank: Community, but not with invertebrates.
Food: All 'meaty' foods.
Compatibility: Usually peaceful but intolerant of its own kind. Its constant activity may worry other less boisterous species.
Availability: Frequently available (wild-caught).
Captive breeding: No information.

FAMILY: LABRIDAE (WRASSES)

The brilliant yellow coloration, coupled with the shape of the body, should leave nobody in doubt as to the inspiration for this species' popular name. It has three black spots on the dorsal fin and one on the caudal peduncle. This helps to distinguish it from a similar-looking species, *H. leucoxanthus*, known as the canary-top wrasse, in which only the top half of the body is yellow; the lower half is silvery-white.

▶ *Fishkeeping data*

Number per aquarium: Two to three.
Community/species tank: Community, but not with invertebrates.
Swimming area: Middle and lower levels.
Food: All 'meaty foods'.
Compatibility: Usually peaceful, but may quarrel amongst themselves.
Availability: Frequently available (wild-caught).
Captive breeding: No information.

▶ **Origins**

From Christmas Island to Marshall Islands, south Japan to southeastern Australia.

Japan

Marshall Islands

Christmas Island

Think ahead

Many of the wrasse family are attractive fishes in their juvenile forms, but become quite large, outgrowing their living quarters and losing their colours as they mature. This is something to bear in mind when selecting wrasses for your collection.

FAMILY: LABRIDAE (WRASSES)

The body shape of this species is one of classic symmetry, with the dorsal and ventral profiles mirroring each other perfectly. The coloration consists of horizontal stripes of alternating yellow and purple. The dorsal and caudal fins are yellow, while the pelvic and anal fins are purple. There is a white-edged black spot on the caudal peduncle. Despite the fish's attractive features, it tends to shy away from exhibiting them, preferring to frequent the coral branches rather than more open water.

The several rows of horizontal stripes makes this fish both attractive and easily recognisable.

▶ Origins

Red Sea to Tuamotu Islands, Ryukyu Islands to Lord Howe Island.

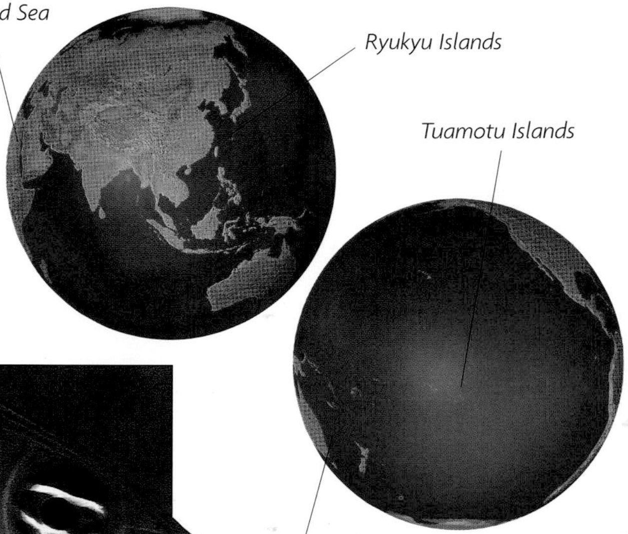

Red Sea

Ryukyu Islands

Tuamotu Islands

Lord Howe Island

▶ Fishkeeping data

Number per aquarium: Two to three.
Community/species tank: Community, but not with invertebrates.
Swimming area: Middle and lower levels.
Food: All 'meaty' foods.
Compatibility: Usually peaceful but may quarrel amongst themselves.
Availability: Frequently available (wild-caught).
Captive breeding: No information.

Surgeonfishes & tangs

Members of the Family Acanthuridae have oval or disc-shaped bodies, edged with long-based dorsal and anal fins. The head has a steeply rising forehead with the eyes mounted high up. The aptly named surgeonfishes carry an erectile scalpel on each side of the caudal peduncle, which can be used either offensively or defensively.

Members of this group are usually active during daylight hours and mostly herbivorous, requiring a good proportion of vegetable matter in their diet. Most are intolerant of their own kind, especially those of similar colours or shapes, but in a large aquarium, it is possible that oval-shaped fish will co-exist with the disc-shaped species without constant quarrelling.

The popular name of 'tang' is likely to be an abbreviation of the German 'seetang', meaning seaweed. This reflects the fishes' fondness for consuming large quantities of algae and kelp as its natural diet. In addition to offering such a diet, it is also important to provide a flow of well-oxygenated water by means of a powerful filtration system with, perhaps, extra aeration.

Above: *With single protruding 'horns' growing from their foreheads, it is no wonder that these Naso species are also described as unicornfish. They need ample swimming space in the aquarium.*

FAMILY: ACANTHURIDAE (SURGEONFISHES AND TANGS)

The steeply rising forehead and oval body are typical of the genus. Furthermore, the black head, white throat and blue body surrounded by yellow dorsal and anal fins, plus a black-decorated caudal fin make recognition of this species easy. The 'scalpel' is disguised in the yellow background of the caudal peduncle. The small, pointed mouth, well-equipped with teeth, is set well forward for efficient grazing on algae or capturing planktonic food. Although the fish often occur in large colonies in nature, most aquatic dealers separate young specimens from one another as they have a penchant for squabbling. Powder blues (and the related powder brown, *A. japonicus*) have a wide distribution area.

When buying surgeons and tangs, look out for 'pinched-in' bodies, especially in the head region. These fishes are constantly eating in the wild and need adequate, vegetable-based diets.

> ### Fishkeeping data

Number per aquarium: One.
Community/species tank: Community.
Swimming area: All levels.
Food: Will accept most foods, including 'meaty' types, but benefits mostly from a high vegetable matter content in its diet. Forages for food continuously.
Compatibility: Quarrelsome with its own kind, but usually ignores invertebrates.
Availability: Usually available (wild-caught).
Captive breeding: No information.

Despite the fish's overall 'blueness', the scalpel is visible against its bright yellow border.

> ### Origins

From East Africa to southwest Indonesia.

East Africa

Indonesia

ORANGE-SPINE UNICORNFISH ● *Naso lituratus*

FAMILY: ACANTHURIDAE (SURGEONFISHES AND TANGS)

Although this species is technically classified as a surgeonfish in most literature, it is also known as a member of the unicornfish group (Nasinae), some of which have a single hornlike projection from the forehead. Additionally, the 'scalpels' are permanently erected and are arranged as a pair of bony projections on each side of the caudal peduncle.

The body coloration is olive-brown, while the whitish face has black markings and bright red lips that account for the fish's popular name of lipstick tang. The long-based dorsal fin is bright yellow and the almost equally long anal fin is brown. There is a black border around the caudal fin. As may be surmised by its size, it is an ocean-going species and naturally requires adequate aquarium space to contain its constant movements.

Fishkeeping data

Number per aquarium: One.
Community/species tank: Community.
Swimming area: All levels.
Food: Will accept most foods, including 'meaty' types, but benefits mostly from a high-vegetable matter content in its diet. Forages for food continuously.
Compatibility: Quarrelsome with its own kind but usually ignores invertebrates.
Availability: Usually available (wild-caught).
Captive breeding: No information.

Origins

From the Red Sea to Hawaii, Japan to the Great Barrier Reef.

Red Sea

Japan

Hawaii

Great Barrier Reef

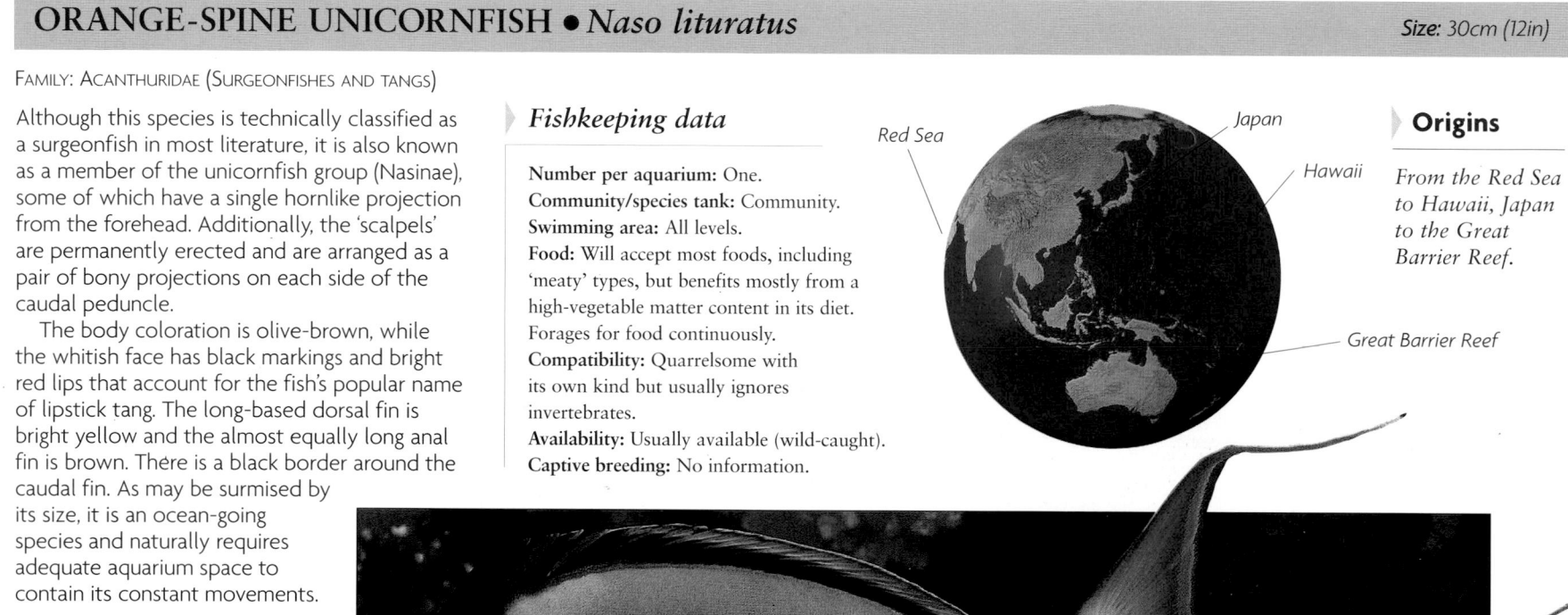

The facial markings of this fish would do credit to any make-up artist, although the demarcations of the body markings are equally well-defined.

FAMILY: ACANTHURIDAE (SURGEONFISHES AND TANGS)

This aquarium favourite is easily identified by its royal blue body, decorated with the familiar painter's palette outline, and the bright yellow caudal and pectoral fins.

All surgeons and tangs are very dependent on well-oxygenated water and are also warmth-loving; a temperature of 26-28°C (79-82°F) suits them fine. Keep the specific gravity as near to the level they would experience in nature and also ensure that the pH is consistently stable at about 8.3.

Like all members of this family, they can be territorially minded, so adequate tank space with plenty of retreats is called for.

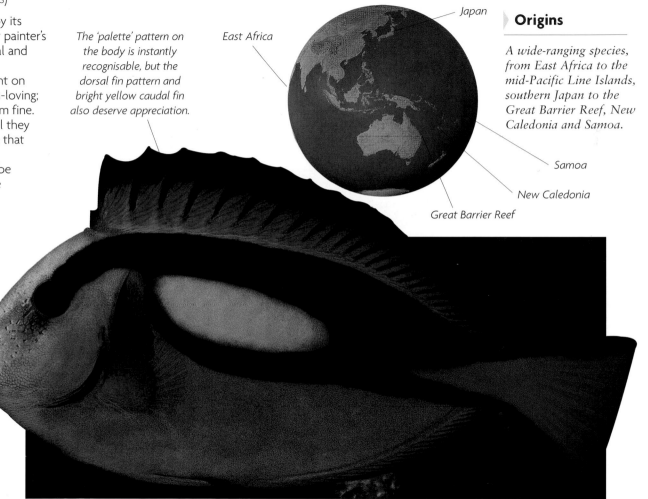

The 'palette' pattern on the body is instantly recognisable, but the dorsal fin pattern and bright yellow caudal fin also deserve appreciation.

Japan
East Africa
Samoa
New Caledonia
Great Barrier Reef

Origins

A wide-ranging species, from East Africa to the mid-Pacific Line Islands, southern Japan to the Great Barrier Reef, New Caledonia and Samoa.

Fishkeeping data

Number per aquarium: One.
Community/species tank: Community.
Swimming area: All levels.
Food: Will accept most foods, including 'meaty' types, but benefits mostly from a high-vegetable matter content in its diet. Forages for food continuously.
Compatibility: Quarrelsome with its own kind, but usually ignores invertebrates.
Availability: Usually available (wild-caught).
Captive breeding: No information.

YELLOW TANG • *Zebrasoma flavescens*

FAMILY: ACANTHURIDAE (SURGEONFISHES AND TANGS)

This brightly coloured yellow fish has a high profile and stands out well in the aquarium. It relishes vegetable matter and will happily munch on scalded lettuce leaves. These can be conveniently secured between the jaws of a magnetic algae-scraper to anchor them into an 'easy-eating' position.

This species cannot be confused with other all-yellow fishes, such as the lemonpeel angelfish *(Centropyge flavissimus)*, Herald's angelfish *(C. heraldi)* or even the related juvenile mimic surgeonfish *(Acanthurus pyroferus)*, because of its distinguishing tall finnage and more laterally compressed body.

This is a fine specimen of yellow tang. Avoid tangs with concave bodies, especially in the head and dorsal areas.

▶ Fishkeeping data

Number per aquarium: One.
Community/species tank: Community.
Swimming area: Middle and lower levels.
Food: Will accept most foods, including 'meaty' types, but benefits mostly from a high-vegetable matter content in its diet. Forages for food continuously.
Compatibility: Quarrelsome with its own kind, but usually ignores invertebrates.
Availability: Usually available (wild-caught).
Captive breeding: No information.

▶ Origins

From Ryukyu Islands eastwards, although most frequently found around Hawaii.

Hawaii

Ryukyu
Islands

Algae-eaters

Keeping a tang in your aquarium is an ideal way of keeping unwanted growths of algae under control. However, some macro-algae is beneficial, as it removes nitrates and adds trace elements.

SAILFIN TANG ● *Zebrasoma veliferum*

FAMILY: ACANTHURIDAE (SURGEONFISHES AND TANGS)

At first glance, this species is reminiscent of the freshwater discus, *Symphysodon* sp, but a closer look will reveal that the actual body shape is not round but a tapering, forward-sloping oval. It is the large, wide dorsal and anal fins that add the illusory 'roundness.'

The pale cream background colour is crossed vertically by five or six brown bars, the darkest two of which are found at the front, crossing the eye and the gill cover. Some bars also carry gold-red streaking along their lengths. The fins repeat the alternate brown-and-cream patterning in what appears as almost concentric circles around the body. The caudal peduncle is light blue with a dark blue scalpel; the caudal fin is yellow. Juveniles, which are yellow with alternating dark bars, frequent shallower waters than adults.

▶ Fishkeeping data

Number per aquarium: One.
Community/species tank: Community
Swimming area: Middle and lower levels.
Food: Will accept most foods, including 'meaty' types, but benefits mostly from a high-vegetable matter content in its diet. Forages for food continuously
Compatibility: Quarrelsome with its own kind, but usually ignores invertebrates.
Availability: Usually available (wild-caught).
Captive breeding: No information.

▶ Origins

From Indonesia to Hawaii, southern Japan to the Great Barrier Reef, New Caledonia and Rapa Island.

Japan

Hawaii

Rapa Island

Great Barrier Reef

New Caledonia

Buying size

All marine fish offered for sale are juveniles. When buying tangs, it is best to avoid some species, such as Acanthurus, if they are less than 7.5cm (3in) long. However, members of the Zebrasoma genus appear to be quite hardy and can be acclimatised to the aquarium below this size.

Triggerfishes

Members of the Family Balistidae have deep, triangular, tapering bodies, with only rudimentary stumps where the pelvic fins would normally emerge. However, their main characteristic is the locking action found on the first of the two dorsal fins. The second spine of the first dorsal fin locks it up into a vertical position, which can effectively lodge the fish into a crevice or, alternatively, prevent it being swallowed by another larger fish. (Remember that it may also catch in the fishkeeper's net!) The first dorsal fin can only be unlocked by releasing the 'trigger', thus allowing the fin to settle back into a groove on the back of the fish, where it is normally carried flat and out of sight until needed.

Do not keep these fish with invertebrates on which they prey in nature. In captivity, they are often quite quarrelsome amongst themselves, so are best kept as single specimens. They have a rather unusual swimming action, propelling themselves through the water using a side-to-side action of their dorsal and anal fins, rather than their tails. In nature, breeding occurs on the seabed, where eggs are deposited in shallow pits dug out by the male fish.

Above: *Many triggerfish have disruptive coloration, the patterning on the body effectively disguising the traditional fish 'outline'. The moustache triggerfish,* Balistoides viridescens, *is a typical example.*

FAMILY: BALISTIDAE (TRIGGERFISHES)

Like many marine species, the clown triggerfish has very disruptive colour patterning. The lower half of the dark body is covered with large white ovals, while the upper body immediately beneath the dorsal fin has a bright-yellow 'saddle'. The eye is hidden, but a bright-yellow stripe crosses the snout below it. The mouth is accentuated by a bright-yellow surround and an additional white line beyond it. The teeth are very sharp, so handle this fish with care. Although triggerfishes have two separate dorsal fins, the first fin is normally folded flat and carried in a groove immediately above the yellow saddle marking.

Right: *Note the 'waviness' of the rear dorsal and anal fins; these are providing propulsion rather than the caudal fin.*

Origins

The clown triggerfish has a wide natural distribution, frequenting waters as far apart as East Africa to Samoa, Japan to Lord Howe Island.

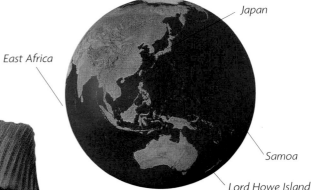

Japan

East Africa

Samoa

Lord Howe Island

Fishkeeping data

Number per aquarium: One.
Community/species tank: Community, with larger fishes but not invertebrates. Often best kept as individuals in a species aquarium.
Swimming area: Middle and lower levels.
Food: All 'meaty' foods.
Compatibility: Territorial.
Availability: Frequently available (wild-caught).
Captive breeding: No information.

REDTOOTH TRIGGERFISH ● *Odonus niger*

FAMILY: BALISTIDAE (TRIGGERFISHES)

The body is a uniform dark blue-green, with the dark-centred scales creating a reticulated effect. The head region may be a shade or two lighter. Some facial markings may be visible, running from the snout up towards the eye. As the common name implies, the teeth are bright red. The outer margins of the fins are a bright blue, and the caudal fin is often very well produced, giving the fish a lyretail appearance. In the wild, when frightened, this is the only part of the fish to be seen, as it dashes into a coral crevice for shelter, leaving its tail sticking out. It is generally considered to be a peaceful species in the aquarium.

▶ Origins

From the Red Sea eastwards to the Society Islands, Japan southwards to the Great Barrier Reef.

You may have to look carefully to see the blue margins on the constantly moving dorsal and anal fins.

Japan

Red Sea

Great Barrier Reef

Society Islands

▶ *Fishkeeping data*

Number per aquarium: One.
Community/species tank: Community, with larger fishes but not invertebrates. Often best kept as individuals in a species aquarium.
Swimming area: All levels.
Food: All 'meaty' foods.
Compatibility: Territorial.
Availability: Frequently available (wild-caught).
Captive breeding: No information.

PICASSOFISH or HUMUHUMU ● *Rhinecanthus aculeatus*

FAMILY: BALISTIDAE (TRIGGERFISHES)

With a native common name almost as bizarre as its colour patterning, this species always invites attention. Although the mouth is relatively small, the yellow lips and elongated yellow line that runs horizontally rearwards across the gill cover give the impression of an immense gape – maybe a defensive coloration? The top of the head is yellowish, the throat and ventral area white. The lower half of the body from the pectoral fins to the caudal peduncle is decorated with diagonal alternate stripes of white and black. The caudal peduncle itself has horizontal black-and-white lines. A blue-edged dark stripe straddles the eye and covers the rear edge of the gill cover, while the upper half of the body is creamy white. The dorsal surface is separated from the diagonal stripes by brown-grey smudges through which brown stripes rise to meet the rearward of the two dorsal fins.

Despite appearances, the Picassofish's mouth is quite small. Note this fish's erect dorsal fin, which is not often seen.

▶ Origins

Indo-Pacific waters from East Africa to Hawaii, Japan to Lord Howe Island.

Japan

Hawaii

East Africa

Lord Howe Island

▶ Fishkeeping data

Number per aquarium: One.
Community/species tank: Community, with larger fishes but not invertebrates. Often best as individuals in a species tank.
Swimming area: Middle and lower levels.
Food: All 'meaty' foods
Compatibility: Territorial.
Availability: Frequently available (wild-caught).
Captive breeding: No information.

Groupers & basslets

The Family Serranidae is very large, containing both brilliantly coloured, modest-sized specimens and drab-coloured monsters of the deep. Body shape tends to be stockily cylindrical, with spiny dorsal fins.

Many members are bottom-loving fish that constantly patrol the rubble at the base of coral reefs, while others may lie in wait, ready to pounce on any passing 'meal'. Sex reversal is common, with a female likely to change into a male as the need occurs, say, should the dominant male of a group of fishes cease to fulfil his function for whatever reason.

With the larger specimens, the production of large amounts of waste material demands an efficient filtration system and more frequent partial water changes to keep water conditions at their optimum.

The smaller specimens are especially suitable for the home aquarium. Such species include the royal gramma and its lookalike royal dottyback, both of which make excellent and highly colourful reef tank inhabitants. Whilst they are included within this section for convenience, they are not strictly serranids but are actually members of the Grammidae and Pseudochromidae families respectively.

Above: *Huge shoals of these wreckfish* (Pseudanthias squamipinnis) *are a common sight in their native habitat. Most will be females in a 'harem' with their attendant solitary, dominant male.*

PANTHERFISH ● *Cromileptes altivelis*

FAMILY: SERRANIDAE (GROUPERS AND BASSLETS)

Despite its large size, there is something very graceful about this species as it cruises slowly around its necessarily large aquarium. The creamy-white body and fins are covered with black spots, which give rise to the alternative popular name of polkadot grouper. Yet another name, the humpbacked grouper, is inspired by the smallness of the head, which accentuates the height of the dorsal profile. Juvenile forms have larger black blotches that become smaller but more numerous with increasing adulthood.

In its natural home, this species is a valued food fish. Despite its apparently small mouth, it would be prudent not to keep it with small fishes, just to be on the safe side.

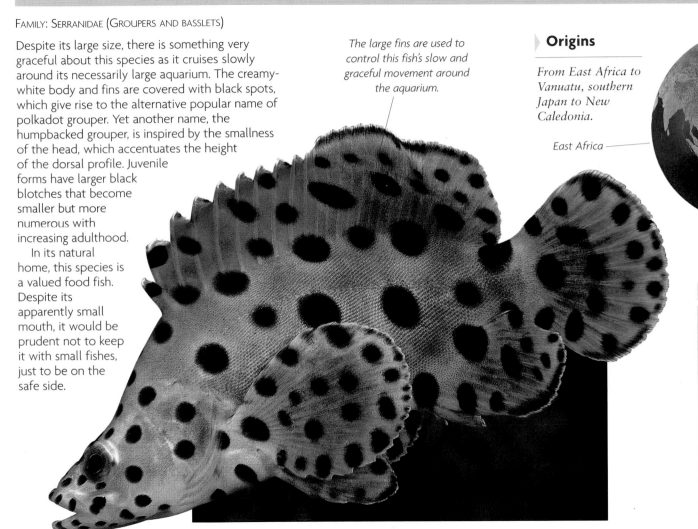

The large fins are used to control this fish's slow and graceful movement around the aquarium.

Origins

From East Africa to Vanuatu, southern Japan to New Caledonia.

Japan

East Africa

Vanuatu

New Caledonia

Fishkeeping data

Number per aquarium: One.
Community/species tank: Community.
Swimming area: All levels.
Food: Prepared foods, including dried and frozen products. Live foods (goldfish, bait fish, etc.) might give them ideas above their station with regard to other tankmates.
Compatibility: Reasonably well-mannered with other suitably sized fishes.
Availability: Frequently available (wild-caught).
Captive breeding: No information.

FAMILY: GRAMMIDAE (GROUPERS AND BASSLETS)

This is one of the most brilliantly coloured fishes to come from the Western Atlantic and Caribbean waters. The body boasts two highly contrasting colours: bright cerise on the front half and an equally bright yellow to the rear. A thin black line runs from the snout upwards through the eye, and there is a black dot at the front of the long-based dorsal fin. The pectoral and pelvic fins are cerise, the caudal fin is bright yellow, and the dorsal and anal fins share both colours.

   Gramma loreto shares its waters with a lookalike species, the bicolor basslet *(Liopropoma klayi)*, in which the cerise colour is confined to the head region. It also lacks the eyestripe and dorsal fin dot. The royal gramma is far more frequently confused with the royal dottyback *(Pseudochromis paccagnellae)* from Indonesian and Pacific waters. Its two similar colours are separated by a hardly discernible thin white line (see page 47).

Breeding

Although eggs are apparently deposited in algae-strewn sites, one report concerning captive breeding cites the fish as mouth-incubating. This may account for the fact that little spawning action has been observed in the wild.

Fishkeeping data

Number per aquarium: One, but established pairs could be kept in very large tanks.
Community/species tank: Community.
Swimming area: Middle and lower levels.
Food: Most foods, including live brineshrimp.
Compatibility: Peaceful, but can be territorial.
Availability: Usually available (wild-caught, but tank-bred numbers increasing).
Captive breeding:
Possible.

Origins

The Bahamas, Venezuela, Lesser Antilles but not Florida.

Bahamas

Lesser Antilles

Venezuela

Below: G. melacara *(10cm/4in) is cerise with some black. This shy fish prefers to stay within easy reach of safe hideaways in crevices on the reef, and is happy resting upside-down against the ceiling of a cave.*

SWISS GUARD BASSLET ● *Liopropoma rubre*

FAMILY: SERRANIDAE (GROUPERS AND BASSLETS)

How quick we are to assign descriptive names to fishes without giving too much thought to their suitability! This species, for example, with its alternating stripes of reddish brown and yellow arranged horizontally along the body obviously reminded its describer of the colours of the uniform of the Papal Swiss Guard in the Vatican City (even though their stripes go vertically!). There are two dorsal fins, the second of which, like the anal fin, carries a black dot. The caudal fin has black areas in its two shallow lobes, smartly terminating the striped patterning of the body.

Although it is common in its native habitat, being a secretive species, it is not actually seen very often.

▶ Fishkeeping data

Number per aquarium: Two to three.
Community/species tank: Community.
Swimming area: Middle and lower levels.
Food: All foods.
Compatibility: Generally peaceful.
Availability: Often available (wild-caught).
Captive breeding: No information.

Florida

Yucatan

Venezuela

▶ Origins

Florida, Yucatan and Venezuela.

The slim body form makes 'crevice-creeping' an easy task.

The two dark markings on the lobes of the caudal fin are connected.

LYRETAIL ANTHIAS, WRECKFISH or GOLDIE • *Pseudanthias squamipinnis*

FAMILY: SERRANIDAE (GROUPERS AND BASSLETS)

This very large genus, containing many species, occurs in massive numbers in the wild, usually with a multitude of females acting as a harem to a very few males. If the dominant male is removed from such a group, another female will change sex to fill the gap. The Midas blenny *(Ecsenius midas)* uses its similar colouring to associate within the shoal for safety.

The body of the female fish is a golden-orange, with a pink-cerise stripe running from the eye rearwards and downwards across the gill cover. The fins are a golden-yellow. The male fish is more of a violet-pink with a reddish head. The gill cover decoration is yellow, and the edges of each fin are purple. The dorsal fin has an elongated third ray and the caudal fin is produced at each tip to form a lyretail. Although obviously gregarious in the wild, within the confines of the aquarium there may not be enough room for several fish to live together peacefully, so try keeping a solitary male or just a couple of females.

Fishkeeping data

Number per aquarium: One (more in a spacious species tank).
Community/species tank: Community.
Swimming area: All levels.
Food: Most foods, especially 'meaty' foods and live adult brineshrimp.
Compatibility: Unless the aquarium is large enough to maintain an established 'pecking order' shoal, frequent altercations will occur between rival males.
Availability: Frequently available (wild-caught).
Captive breeding: No information.

Origins

From the Red Sea to the Solomon Islands, south Japan to New South Wales.

The male has an elongated third ray on the dorsal fin and a lyre-shaped caudal fin.

Japan

Red Sea

Solomon Islands

New South Wales

FAMILY: PSEUDOCHROMIDAE (GROUPERS AND BASSLETS)

This brilliantly coloured species is almost a replica of the royal gramma *(Gramma loreto,* see page 44). However, it is not quite so striking, as its dorsal and anal fins are colourless, and there is no black eyestripe. The giveaway clue to positive identification is the thin white line that runs vertically downwards across the body to separate the cerise and yellow areas. It is similar in habit to the basslets, keeping close to the sea wall on reefs and swimming slowly over coral rubble in its native waters.

Below: *Look for the fine white line separating the two main body colours. This feature distinguishes the fish from the very similar* Gramma loreto.

▶ Origins

From Indonesia to Papua New Guinea, Sulawesi, Vanuatu and northern Australia.

Papua New Guinea

Sulawesi

Vanuatu

▶ *Fishkeeping data*

Number per aquarium: One, but established pairs could be kept in very large tanks.

Community/species tank: Community or spacious species tank.

Swimming area: Middle and lower levels.

Food: Most foods, especially fresh or frozen 'meaty' foods.

Compatibility: Very territorial.

Availability: Often available (wild-caught, but tank-bred numbers increasing).

Captive breeding: Occasionally reported, but problems may occur with raising any resulting fry.

Blennies & gobies

Members of the Blenniidae and Gobiidae Families share many characteristics. All are small, cylindrical fish that inhabit the seabed. Generally carnivorous, they constantly dash about in search of a meal, but are always ready to rush back to the sanctuary of a nearby cave or pile of rocks should they feel threatened.

Outwardly, they could be mistaken for members of the same family, but closer examination reveals quite distinct differences. Blennies generally have a continuous, long-based dorsal fin, whereas gobies have two separate dorsal fins. Another characteristic is that blennies have separate pelvic fins, while in gobies these are fused together to form a suction disc with which the fish anchor themselves into position. A further aid to positive identification is that some blennies have 'cirri' – peculiar eyebrowlike growths on the head that gobies lack.

Several gobies have been bred in captivity. Many species live in substrate burrows and some even share these homes with invertebrates, such as pistol shrimps. A number of blennies are mimics; some, such as the Midas blenny (*Ecsenius midas*), in order to associate with other fishes for safety reasons, others for more ulterior motives (especially the sabre-tooth blenny, *Aspidontus taeniatus*, which mimics the cleanerfish in order to procure a quick meal!) Always choose carefully before you buy.

The similarly shaped dartfishes have been included in this section for convenience, although they strictly belong to the Family Microdesmidae and, unlike either blennies or gobies, spend more time away from the substrate area of the aquarium. They are easily distinguished by the very long extended rays in the dorsal fin.

Above: *Protected by a bitter-tasting, predator-deterring mucus, the citron goby* (Gobiodon citrinus) *regularly ventures above the substrate areas so beloved by other members of the family.*

FAMILY: BLENNIIDAE (BLENNIES)

The popular name of this species could, conceivably, be taken in two ways: either as a straightforward description of the two-part coloration of the body, or as a reference to the various colour phases seen in the fish. In general, the front half of the body is dark blue and brown and the rear portion is bright yellow. The two sections of the continuous dorsal fin correspond in colour to the part of the body they adjoin, while the anal and caudal fins are yellow. Two curly 'eyebrows' appear in front of the eyes.

Variations in colour include an all-brown form, and a dark-topped body with silvery blue lower flanks separated by a horizontal white band. The caudal fin and most rearward section of the body are yellow. Further colour variations occur during spawning, when the male turns red with white transverse bars, and the female becomes yellow.

Fishkeeping data

Number per aquarium: One – maybe more in a separate, spacious species tank.
Community/species tank: Quiet community tank or species tank with plenty of hideaways.
Swimming area: Substrate level.
Food: All foods.
Compatibility: Shy and peaceful; do not keep with larger fishes.
Availability: Generally available (wild-caught).
Captive breeding: No information.

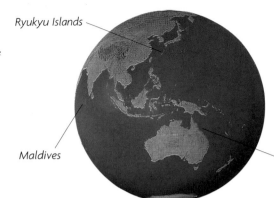

Ryukyu Islands

Maldives

Great Barrier Reef

Origins

From the Maldives, eastwards and northwards to the Ryukyu Islands and south to the Great Barrier Reef.

The body colours of male and female may be variable, as both change colour at breeding time.

SMITH'S FANG BLENNY ● *Meiacanthus smithi*

FAMILY: BLENNIIDAE (BLENNIES)

This very smart fish has a smoky-grey-blue body topped with a white-edged, dark blue dorsal fin. The anal fin is blue. Unlike some members of the genus, the black-streaked caudal fin is rounded and not lyre-shaped. There is a diagonal blue-edged black band running upwards through the eye.

This genus is far more adventurous than most blennies; because it has a fully-functional swimbladder, it can venture up into midwater with greater ease than its more substrate-bound relatives.

Another fang blenny (*Plagiotremus phenax*) is a mimic of this species, but can be differentiated from *M. smithi* by the slightly broader dorsal fin with a more rounded front, a black-edged anal fin and a squared-off caudal fin. It lacks the eye-bar. This differentiation is vital, because whereas *M. smithi* is a peaceful species, *P. phenax* is definitely not.

Sharp teeth

When they leave the relative safety of the substrate, this group of fishes is less likely to be predated upon because they have canine teeth, from which they derive not only protection, but also their popular name of fang, or sabre-tooth, blennies.

▶ Origins

From the Maldives in the Indian Ocean to western Indonesia.

Maldives

Western Indonesia

▶ Fishkeeping data

Number per aquarium: One.
Community/species tank: Quiet community or species tank.
Swimming area: Middle and lower levels.
Food: Most foods.
Compatibility: Peaceful, despite its sinister-sounding popular name.
Availability: Often available (wild-caught).
Captive breeding: No information.

The diagonal stripe through the eye is one identifying feature. Another is the rounded — not lyre-shaped — caudal fin.

FAMILY: GOBIIDAE (GOBIES)

The blue-grey body is crossed vertically by seven orange-red bands. The two dorsal fins are yellow, the foremost one having a dark ocellus, or 'eyespot', at its base. The pectoral, pelvic, anal and caudal fins are the same colour as the body.

This body colour and patterning is shared by several other species, including Steinitz' prawn goby (*A. steinitzi*), which has a dark area above the mouth and no dorsal fin eyespot, and Magnus' prawn goby (*A. sungami*), which has plain fins and no dark area.

Spotted prawn goby

Members of this genus live in burrows with a shrimp or prawn of the Alphaeid group. Since these invertebrates are usually blind or only partially sighted, the association works well; the prawn digs the burrow, the fish acts as lookout. The creamy-yellow body of A. guttata (below) is covered with reddish brown spots that extend into the dorsal, anal and caudal fins.

▶ Origins

From the Moluccas eastwards to the Solomon Islands, Ryukyu Islands south to the Great Barrier Reef.

Ryukyu Islands

Moluccas

Great Barrier Reef

Solomon Islands

▶ *Fishkeeping data*

Number per aquarium: One.
Community/species tank: Community or species tank with a sufficiently deep substrate to accommodate burrowing.
Swimming area: Substrate level.
Food: Meaty foods.
Compatibility: Peaceful.
Availability: Often available (wild-caught).
Captive breeding: No information.

OLD GLORY or RAINFORD'S GOBY • *Amblygobius rainfordi*

Size: Males 6.5cm (2.5in)

FAMILY: GOBIIDAE (GOBIES)

This species is very reminiscent of the Swiss Guard basslet (*Liopropoma rubre*, page 45) in its coloration, but the body ground colour is a greenish yellow and the red horizontal stripes are much thinner. Two dark ocelli appear, one at the base of the second dorsal fin and another at the top tip of the caudal peduncle. The first dorsal fin and the anal, pectoral and pelvic fins are clear. The body shape is less blunt-headed than that of *L. rubre* and its symmetrical dorsal and ventral profiles indicate that it may spend as much time in midwater as on the substrate.

Brown-barred goby

The heavily built, streamlined body of *A. phalaena* has a greenish grey background crossed by alternating vertical bands of brown and white. It grows to 15cm (6in) and lives in western Pacific waters, from Sumatra to the Great Barrier Reef and New South Wales.

Origins

From the Philippines southwards to northwestern Australia and the Great Barrier Reef.

Great Barrier Reef

Philippines

Northwestern Australia

Fishkeeping data

Number per aquarium: One.

Community/species tank: Community, or species tank with a sufficiently deep substrate to accommodate burrowing.

Swimming area: Middle and lower levels.

Food: Meaty foods.

Compatibility: Peaceful.

Availability: Often available (wild-caught).

Captive breeding: No information.

CITRON GOBY or CORAL GOBY • *Gobiodon citrinus*

FAMILY: GOBIIDAE (GOBIES)

As its popular name implies, the body and fin colour is a lemon-yellow; only the dorsal surface is a slightly darker shade. However, this plainness is alleviated by the addition of brilliant electric-blue streaks – lines along the bases of the dorsal and anal fins, two downward diagonal streaks across the rear of the gill cover and two further streaks radiating down from the eye. However, this species is variable in colour and reports suggest that overall green or brown specimens occur.

This species has two distinguishing characteristics. Firstly, unlike most gobies, it is not a bottom-dwelling species, preferring to spend its time amongst branches of the coral heads on the reef. This trait is reflected in its alternative popular name. Secondly, it is protected against predation by the bitter-tasting mucus layer covering its skin.

Fishkeeping data

Number per aquarium: One.
Community/species tank: Quiet community or species tank.
Swimming area: Middle or upper levels amongst coral branches.
Food: All foods.
Compatibility: Peaceful and likely to be left alone due to its bitter-tasting mucus covering.
Availability: Generally available (wild-caught and tank-bred).
Captive breeding: Yes.

Breeding

Eggs are laid in caves, under overhanging rocks or in considerately placed lengths of plastic pipe. The fertilised eggs are guarded by the male until the fry are free-swimming.

Origins

From the Red Sea eastwards to Samoa, from Japan south to the Great Barrier Reef.

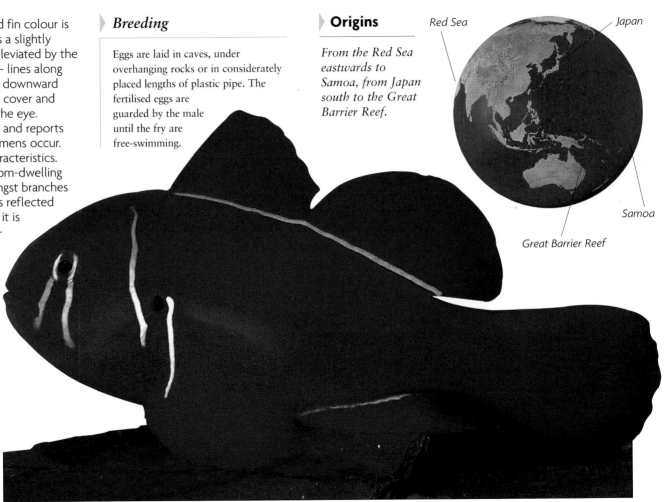

Red Sea

Japan

Samoa

Great Barrier Reef

53

NEON GOBY ● *Gobiosoma oceanops*

FAMILY: GOBIIDAE (GOBIES)

Despite the growing numbers of gobies becoming available in the hobby, the neon goby remains one of the most popular, although it could be classed as a veteran.

The dark blue body, with a white underside, is highlighted by a glowing electric-blue line running from the snout the whole length of the body. Such a simple design, yet so attractive. The species – one among a number of so-called cleaner gobies in the genus – can be distinguished from similar species by the gap on the snout between the two blue lines. In other species, the lines may be joined across the snout or have a 'pip' marking in the gap.

In nature, this goby sits in crevices or caves waiting for food or, perhaps, a customer for its cleaning services. Its coloration is reminiscent of the cleaner wrasse *(Labroides dimidiatus)* and it has been known to 'clean' divers' hands.

Unfortunately, although the neon goby makes an excellent aquarium subject, being hardy and easy to keep and breed, it is rather shortlived. If you want to have them for a reasonable time, it is best to buy several juveniles rather than just one or two obviously adult fish.

Breeding

One of the earliest gobies to be bred in captivity. It lays its eggs in holes in rocks, in vacant 'tubes' of feather-duster worms, plastic pipes or on any convenient firm surface. The male guards the eggs. Once the fry are free-swimming, they develop quite rapidly and appear to mature within a few months.

Origins

Western Atlantic waters around Florida, Belize and Honduras.

Florida   Atlantic Ocean

Belize

Honduras

Fishkeeping data

Number per aquarium: Two to three.
Community/species tank: Quiet community or species tank with rocky caves.
Swimming area: Substrate level.
Food: All foods.
Compatibility: Peaceful and maybe even bold with larger fish.
Availability: Generally available (tank-bred).
Captive breeding: Long-standing aquarium-bred species.

FAMILY: GOBIIDAE (GOBIES)

Understandably, this gorgeously coloured goby is a long-standing aquarium favourite. The body is a glowing red, overlaid with a number of vertical bright blue stripes. The first few rays of the first dorsal fin are elongated. There is a similar-looking species *(L. pulchellus)*, but its body is not quite such a deep red and it has more vertical stripes.

It might be said that this fish is the equivalent (in terms of its lifespan) of many of the freshwater killifishes, living, as it does, not much longer than a year or so. As its natural home is quite a distance northwards from that of most 'tropical' marine species, it does not require quite such a high water temperature, which would probably shorten its naturally brief life even more.

▶ Fishkeeping data

Number per aquarium: Two or three.
Community/species tank: Quiet community or species tank.
Swimming area: Substrate level.
Food: Meaty foods, but prefers small live foods.
Compatibility: Peaceful, although it can be territorial amongst its own kind.
Availability: Often available (wild-caught or tank-bred).
Captive breeding: Has been bred in the aquarium.

▶ Origins

Coastal waters off southern California and the Gulf of California.

Southern California

Gulf of California

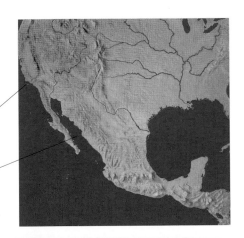

Right: The flat, lower contour of the body indicates that the blue-banded goby spends all its time on the substrate.

▶ Breeding

After a courtship that involves much harassing and nipping of the female by the male, the eggs are finally laid in the chosen secluded site. They are guarded by the male until they hatch.

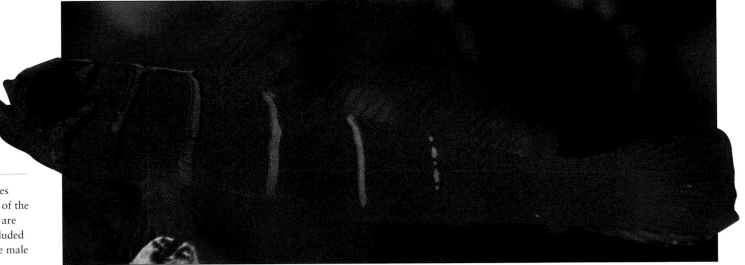

DECORATED DARTFISH or PURPLE FIREFISH ● *Nemateleotris decora*

FAMILY: MICRODESMIDAE (DARTFISHES)

It is no wonder that this genus has become so popular. The fishes' colours (and their willingness to display them) are simply stunning. The creamy-yellow cylindrical body is framed by purple and red finnage, with the first rays of the front dorsal fin carried permanently erect like a banner. A purple mask covers the forehead and is led by a thin line upwards over the back to join the dorsal fin.

Although happy to hover in groups in midwater, where water currents bring their food, these fish also require immediate access to safe boltholes should they feel threatened. An aquarium suitably decorated with rocks is a prerequisite to making these beautiful fishes become settled in captivity.

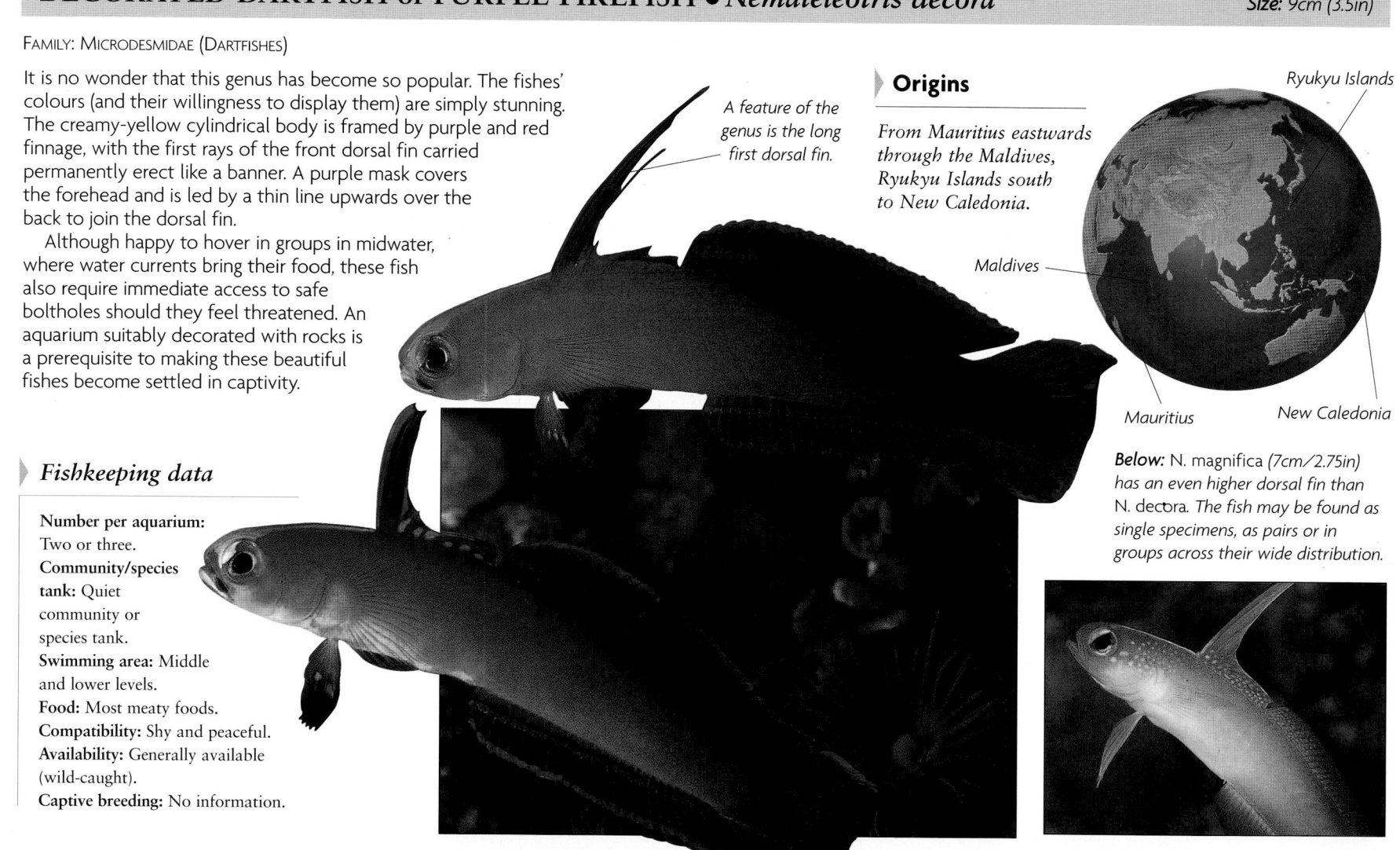

A feature of the genus is the long first dorsal fin.

▶ Origins

From Mauritius eastwards through the Maldives, Ryukyu Islands south to New Caledonia.

Ryukyu Islands

Maldives

Mauritius　　　New Caledonia

Below: N. magnifica (7cm/2.75in) has an even higher dorsal fin than N. decora. The fish may be found as single specimens, as pairs or in groups across their wide distribution.

▶ *Fishkeeping data*

Number per aquarium: Two or three.
Community/species tank: Quiet community or species tank.
Swimming area: Middle and lower levels.
Food: Most meaty foods.
Compatibility: Shy and peaceful.
Availability: Generally available (wild-caught).
Captive breeding: No information.

BLUE STREAK or GOLDEN-HEADED SLEEPER GOBY ● *Valenciennea strigata*

FAMILY: GOBIIDAE (GOBIES)

At first glance, the delicate blue body and yellow head of this species resemble the coloration of the yellow-headed jawfish *(Opisthognathus aurifrons)*. However, the presence of two dorsal fins (the first often carries extended rays in adults) marks the fish as a goby, while the bright blue streak running obliquely upwards across the gill cover is another distinguishing feature.

In nature, a characteristic action of this burrowing, prawn-independent genus is its substrate-chewing, as it sifts through particles searching for tiny worms and crustaceans.

V. strigata is normally classed as a sleeper goby, a group of gobies previously referred to as Eleotridae, and usually regarded as having a sedentary lifestyle. Specimens of this genus also appear to communicate through movements of the mouth. Whether these 'signals' are audible or simply visible signs is not clear.

Fishkeeping data

Number per aquarium: One or an established pair.
Community/species tank: Quiet community or species tank.
Swimming area: Lower levels.
Food: All meaty foods.
Compatibility: Peaceful.
Availability: Generally available (wild-caught).
Captive breeding: No information.

Origins

Lagoons and seaward reefs from East Africa to the Society Islands, Ryukyu Islands south to Lord Howe Island.

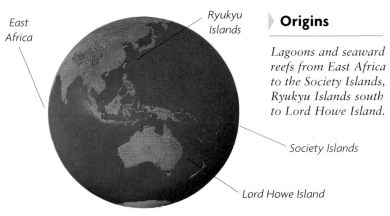

East Africa

Ryukyu Islands

Society Islands

Lord Howe Island

The blue-streaked cheek of this fish makes identification easy.

Boxfishes, cowfishes & pufferfishes

Right: *Male and female spotted boxfishes (Ostracion meleagris) are differently patterned; this is the more colourful male. All the fishes in this group have rigid bodies; only the tail fin is flexible.*

This group of fishes encompasses several families, but we have collected them together for convenience, as they share almost a common body shape and similar physical characteristics.

It is the exterior coverings of these fish that provide the interest. In the boxfishes and cowfishes there is a covering of bony plates that form an exoskeleton. The pufferfishes have two characteristic features: erectile spines and the ability to inflate their bodies to a size that will deter any foes. Some members of this group can further defend themselves when threatened or under stress by releasing self-generated toxins into the water. Handle them with care and always transport specimens alone in their own bag. Should a specimen die unnoticed in the aquarium, it is possible that the whole population of the aquarium will be wiped out as a result of the toxins from the corpse.

Despite all these warnings, do not be left with the impression that these fishes are not suitable inmates for your aquarium. On the contrary, they soon become 'tame' and get to know when it is feeding time. Due to their adult size, only juvenile specimens are likely to be available commercially, which is no bad thing for fishkeepers with modest-sized – and invertebrate-free – tanks.

COWFISH ● *Lactoria cornuta*

FAMILY: OSTRACIIDAE (BOXFISH)

Many aquarium fish are kept for their curiosity value and none is more curious than the cowfish. Here is a fish that wears its skeleton on the outside as a suit of rigid bony plates. The only apparent area for growth is the part of the fish that sticks out from the caudal peduncle. Naturally, the fish gets its popular name from the two 'horns' that project from the top of a square head that rises steeply from a terminal mouth. The mouth is conveniently situated right at the bottom corner of the head, which makes for easy feeding on invertebrates on the substrate. The fish flips them up with a jet of water from its mouth and seizes them as they fall.

Two 'horns' adorn the head of the aptly named cowfish.

▶ Fishkeeping data

Number per aquarium: One.
Community/species tank: Species collection or community with very peaceful and slow-moving tankmates.
Swimming area: Middle and lower levels.
Food: Almost everything; appreciates green matter, plus shellfish. The shells help to keep the teeth worn down.
Compatibility: Do not keep with small fishes or invertebrates.
Availability: Frequently available (wild-caught).
Captive breeding: No information.

▶ Origins

From the Red Sea to the Marquesas and Tuamotu Islands, South Korea, South Japan and to Lord Howe Island.

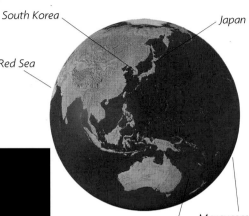

South Korea

Japan

Red Sea

Marquesas Islands

Lord Howe Island

The caudal fin (along with the dorsal fin) is the only 'active' part of the fish, protruding from the bony, boxlike body.

FAMILY: OSTRACIIDAE (BOXFISH)

This species was responsible for much confusion until it was realised that two differently patterned fish were not, in fact, different species, but merely male and female of the same species!

The male has the best coloration, with the two distinct areas of the body being separated by a yellow line. The dorsal surface is black, the area below the yellow line is blue and the body (excluding the blue head) is speckled with black-edged yellow spots. The pelvic fins are missing and propulsion is achieved by the rear-located dorsal and anal fins only. The female has a black body covered with white spots.

In the wild, this species feeds on sponges and bottom-dwelling invertebrates.

The male fish has a two-patterned body.

The female has a uniformly spotted body pattern.

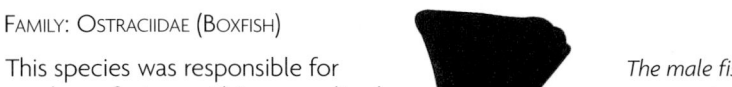

East Africa

Great Barrier Reef

Hawaii

Mexico

Mid-Pacific islands

▶ Origins

East Africa to Mexico via Hawaii, south Japan to the Great Barrier Reef and eastwards to the mid-Pacific islands.

▶ *Fishkeeping data*

Number per aquarium: One.
Community/species tank: Species collection, or community with very peaceful and slow-moving tankmates.
Swimming area: Middle and lower levels.
Food: Almost everything; appreciates green matter, plus shellfish. The shells help to keep the teeth worn down.
Compatibility: Do not keep with small fishes or invertebrates.
Availability: Frequently available (wild-caught).
Captive breeding: No information.

FAMILY: DIODONTIDAE (PORCUPINEFISH)

The body shape is much like a horizontally elongated teardrop, with a slightly flattened, broad top and the large eyes set high up. The yellow body is covered with a series of dark brown stripes, and several large, dark ocelli are distributed over the body. The spines are held erect as a permanent deterrent to would-be predators and this stands the fish in good stead, as it does not inflate itself as do most members of this group. It is not regularly seen at aquatic outlets.

▶ *Fishkeeping data*

Number per aquarium: One.
Community/species tank: Species collection, or community with very peaceful and slow-moving tankmates.
Swimming area: Middle and lower levels.
Food: Almost everything; appreciates green matter, plus shellfish. The shells help to keep the teeth worn down.
Compatibility: Not with small fishes or invertebrates.
Availability: Frequently available (wild-caught).
Captive breeding: No information.

Florida

Brazil

▶ **Origins**

Common in Florida (and occasionally northwards), plus coastal waters south to Brazil (excluding the Caribbean islands).

The relatively shallow body allows the fish to lurk in caves and narrow crevices.

Handle with care

Remember to handle all the porcupinefishes and burrfushes carefully to avoid stressing them, which would cause them to exude toxins and 'self-destruct'. Do not 'net' them (watch out for those spines!) or expose them to the air – they might 'inflate'. It is best to capture them in a water-filled plastic bag.

BALLOONFISH or LONG-SPINED PORCUPINEFISH ● *Diodon holocanthus*

Size: *50cm (20in)*

FAMILY: DIODONTIDAE (PORCUPINEFISH)

The body has a yellowish tinge with a white ventral surface. A number of short dark bars straddle the dorsal surface, while a much longer one covers the eye and gill cover. The dorsal, anal and caudal fins are yellow. A feature of the Diodontidae family is the fusing together of the two front teeth on each jaw ('diodon' meaning two teeth) to form a bony beak with which the fish crushes shelled invertebrates. It is a poor swimmer and its large eyes may denote that it does its feeding more by night than by day.

One problem with all 'inflatable' fish is that they can inflate with air, rather than water, especially if lifted from the water. In such cases, the fish may find it very difficult to deflate itself afterwards.

Faced with prickly spines, plus an almost spherical body when inflated, it is no wonder that predators steer clear of this species.

The two front teeth on each jaw are fused together to form a shell-crushing, bony beak.

▶ Origins

Found worldwide in all warm seas.

Pacific Ocean

Atlantic Ocean

Indian Ocean

▶ *Fishkeeping data*

Number per aquarium: One.
Community/species tank: Species collection, or community with very peaceful and slow-moving tankmates.
Swimming area: Middle and lower levels.
Food: Almost everything; appreciates green matter, plus shellfish. The shells help to keep the teeth worn down.
Compatibility: Not with small fishes or invertebrates.
Availability: Frequently available (wild-caught).
Captive breeding: No information.

BLACK-SADDLED TOBY • *Canthigaster valentini*

FAMILY: TETRAODONTIDAE (PUFFERFISH)

The white body of this fish has unusual coloration imposed upon it. Four dark, triangular blotches appear on the dorsal surface, from the top of the head to the caudal peduncle, the middle two extending down the flanks almost to the ventral surface. Additionally, the lower half of the body is peppered with yellowish brown spots, and the yellow caudal fin has a black top and bottom edge.

Distinctive as it may sound, this patterning is not exclusive to this species. The black saddle filefish *(Paraluteres prionurus)* has exactly the same markings, with the exception of the caudal fin, which lacks the black top and bottom edges.

Males surround themselves with a harem of females with whom they mate on a rotational and regular basis; eggs are laid in a nest of algae.

The dark markings reach further down the body than on the similar-looking species, Canthigaster coronata.

▶ Origins

Wide distribution including the Red Sea to Tuamotu Islands, South Japan to Lord Howe Island.

Red Sea

Tuamotu Islands

Lord Howe Island

▶ *Fishkeeping data*

Number per aquarium: One.
Community/species tank: Species collection, or community with very peaceful and slow-moving tankmates.
Swimming area: Middle and lower levels.
Food: Almost everything; appreciates green matter, plus shellfish. The shells help to keep the teeth worn down.
Compatibility: Not with small fishes or invertebrates.
Availability: Frequently available (wild-caught).
Captive breeding: No information.

63

Miscellaneous marine species

This final section of the book features fish from a number of families. Cardinalfishes (Apogonidae) are ideal for the marine aquarium. They are undemanding, and amenable to aquarium conditions and foods. A common characteristic is the presence of two separate dorsal fins. Hawkfishes (Cirrhitidae) like to perch on a rocky outcrop as they await any passing prey, typical behaviour of species lacking a swimbladder. Hawkfishes should settle down quickly in captivity, but mixing hawkfish species in the tank may lead to quarrels.

The slow-moving lionfishes (Scorpaenidae) present a false picture of serenity. A sudden gulp from the huge mouth can engulf any passing prey and a sting from their venomous spines can seriously incapacitate the careless handler. As these fish are naturally active at dusk and dawn, the aquarium need not be too brightly lit. Filefishes (Monocanthidae) have two dorsal fins, the posterior one being used with the anal fin for propulsion. The skin is rough to the touch and often causes problems when netting; using a plastic bag to capture them is recommended.

Jawfishes (Opisthognathidae) need a reasonably 'quiet' aquarium with peaceful tankmates, and a soft substrate in which they can build a burrow. They normally hover vertically, tail-down, around the burrow entrance into which they can retreat – backwards – like lightning. Dragonets (Callionymidae) are hard to see against the substrate, where they make their permanent living space. They will only really thrive with copious amounts of live foods; do not keep them with any sizeable tankmates who would out-compete them in the hunt for food.

Above: With its venom-filled spines, the lionfish (Pterois volitans) is a favourite public aquarium exhibit, where its graceful drifting form of locomotion belies a more sinister motive – looking for food.

YELLOW-STRIPED CARDINALFISH • *Apogon cyanosoma*

FAMILY: APOGONIDAE (CARDINALFISHES)

True to its common name, the streamlined body carries five or six horizontal yellow lines along the flanks. The eye is large. When the fish is viewed from the side, the pectoral, pelvic and the first (of two) dorsal fins all line up vertically. All the fins are colourless. A similar-looking species, the blue-spot cardinalfish *(A. nitidus)*, is found over much of the same distribution area, but it has a somewhat brown tinge to the yellow areas and a dark line running centrally through the caudal fin.

Cardinalfishes are shoaling fish that rest in caves or under coral heads during daylight hours. After dusk, they use their large eyes to hunt for food.

▶ Origins

Red Sea to the Marshall Islands, south Japan to the Great Barrier Reef.

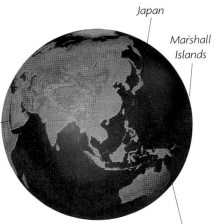

Japan

Marshall Islands

Red Sea

Great Barrier Reef

▶ *Fishkeeping data*

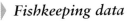

Number per aquarium: Two or three.
Community/species tank: Community, but not with large fishes.
Swimming area: Middle and lower levels.
Food: All 'meaty' foods, fresh or frozen, plus live brineshrimp.
Compatibility: Peaceful, sometimes shy and won't bother other fishes.
Availability: Often available (wild-caught).
Captive breeding: No information.

BANGGAI or BORNEO or HIGHFIN CARDINALFISH • *Pterapogon kauderni*

Size: *8cm (3.2in)*

FAMILY: APOGONIDAE (CARDINALFISHES)

Every so often, a species comes along that finds instant appeal amongst fishkeepers, and so it is with the Banggai cardinalfish. It has striking silver-and-black coloration, very reminiscent of the freshwater angelfish, *Pterophyllum scalare*, with one or two extra adornments. The top and bottom parts of the caudal peduncle have a white-edged black stripe that continues to the tips of the caudal fin. The large pelvic fins, together with the anal fin, seem to mirror the two separate dorsal fins, while the whole body is overlaid with white dots (buyers rest assured, this is not an outbreak of some aquatic ailment!).

Discovered in 1990 in the Banggai Islands of Sulawesi in Indonesia, this fish has proved to be extremely amenable to life in captivity and many public aquariums are able to breed them freely (they are mouthbrooders). This means that future supplies to the aquatic trade should be secure, thus allowing the original wild stock to continue their natural existence without the threat of fish collectors hunting them down.

▶ Origins

The Banggai Islands of Sulawesi in Indonesia.

Banggai Islands

▶ Breeding

Increasingly, this species is being bred in public aquariums. The male undertakes the mouthbrooding duties of the fertilised eggs. Once hatched, the free-swimming fry are able to take newly hatched brineshrimp as a first food.

▶ Fishkeeping data

Number per aquarium: Two or three.
Community/species tank: Species or community, but not with large fishes.
Swimming area: Middle and lower levels.
Food: All 'meaty' foods, fresh or frozen, plus live brineshrimp.
Compatibility: Peaceful, sometimes a little quarrelsome between themselves.
Availability: Recent introduction but plentiful (wild-caught, but soon tank-bred).
Captive breeding: Regularly in public aquariums and probably hobbyists' tanks, too.

FAMILY: APOGONIDAE (CARDINALFISHES)

In common with the previously described species, the body shape of this fish is quite stocky and deep, with the dorsal and ventral contours being quite convex. The patterning is quite unusual in that the dark-spotted rear half of the body is separated from the unadorned front section by a broad, dark brown vertical band. The front dorsal fin has some patterning and the large pelvic fins are yellowish edged with white. The large eye, indicative of a nocturnally active species, is red-rimmed with two vertical white stripes.

The pyjama cardinalfish's body is bizarrely marked with different zones of patterning.

▶ Origins

From Java to Papua New Guinea, and Ryukyu Islands south to Great Barrier Reef.

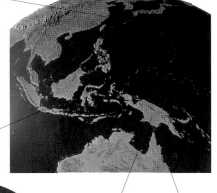

Ryukyu Islands

Java

Papua New Guinea

Great Barrier Reef

▶ *Fishkeeping data*

Number per aquarium: Two or three.
Community/species tank: Community, but not with large fishes.
Swimming area: All levels.
Food: All 'meaty' foods, fresh or frozen, plus live brineshrimp.
Compatibility: Peaceful, shy and sometimes a little quarrelsome between themselves.
Availability: Often available (wild-caught).
Captive breeding: No information, but may occur unnoticed.

LONGNOSED HAWKFISH ● *Oxycirrhites typus*

FAMILY: CIRRHITIDAE (HAWKFISHES)

At one time, this was the only hawkfish likely to be found in dealers' tanks. The long snout and jawline, together with the squares of bright red covering the whitish body, make the longnosed hawkfish instantly recognisable. The long-based dorsal fin has a spiny front section, and tiny growths at the tips of the dorsal spines are often visible. These growths, known as cirri, account for the derivation of the Family name, Cirrhitidae.

This species, along with others in the genus, is not an active fish, spending its time on an outcrop of coral or any suitable aquarium decoration, waiting for a feeding opportunity to present itself. This apparently peaceful occupation may seem innocent enough, but small fishes and non-sedentary invertebrates may be at risk.

▶ Fishkeeping data

Number per aquarium: One.
Community/species tank: Community, but not with very small fishes or invertebrates.
Swimming area: Middle and lower levels.
Food: All foods.
Compatibility: Fairly peaceful, may be territorial; certainly an opportunistic, rather than predatory, feeder.
Availability: Regularly available (wild-caught).
Captive breeding: No information.

▶ Origins

The natural distribution of the longnosed hawkfish ranges from the Red Sea to Panama, including Japan, Hawaii and New Caledonia.

Hawaii

Panama

Red Sea

Japan

New Caledonia

Left: *The flat lower contour of the body makes perching on rocky outcrops easy, as the longnosed hawkfish waits for a passing meal.*

68

FAMILY: FAMILY: CIRRHITIDAE (HAWKFISHES)

With its high, arched back and flatter ventral surface, the body contour of this fish is not entirely symmetrical, but obviously an efficient design for a fish that does not do a lot of swimming around. The head and dorsal surface are red, the flanks below the median line are yellow and separated by a bright white band (not present in all cases) running from mid-dorsal fin to the end of the caudal peduncle. Some radiating, red-edged, blue bands emerge from the rear edge of the gill cover. All the fins are yellow. The species takes its common name from a blue, red and yellow-edged dark area on the head just above, and to the rear of, the eye. Other species share this decoration.

The 'eye patch' is not exclusive to this species, but the white body stripe (when present) helps with positive identification.

On the lookout

The high-set eyes of the hawkfishes enable them to spot potential prey easily. Their body shape is ideally suited to their sedentary life; they prefer their meals to come to them, rather than chase their food.

▶ **Origins**

From East Africa to Hawaii, south Japan to Norfolk Island.

Japan

Hawaii

East Africa

Norfolk Island

▶ *Fishkeeping data*

Number per aquarium: One.
Community/species tank: Community, but not with very small fishes or invertebrates.
Swimming area: Middle and lower levels.
Food: All foods.
Compatibility: Peaceful.
Availability: Often available (wild-caught).
Captive breeding: No information.

FAMILY: SCORPAENIDAE (LIONFISHES)

Such are the proportions of the intricately patterned fins, that it is often hard to determine the exact body shape of these fishes. In fact, the body is sturdily built, with a high dorsal arch and, unsurprisingly for a genus that spends some time around the substrate level of the aquarium, a flattened ventral surface.

Deep reddish brown bands, alternating with lighter brown, cross the body vertically, and this patterning appears to extend concentrically into all fins. The large, fan-shaped pectoral fins have connecting tissue membrane right to the tips of the fin rays. The first few rays of the dorsal fin are separate and there is a pair of 'hornlike' growths above the eyes. A distinguishing characteristic of this species is the dark ocellus spot on the lower part of the gill cover.

Below: *The pectoral fins have much more connecting tissue between the spines than is seen in other species in this family group.*

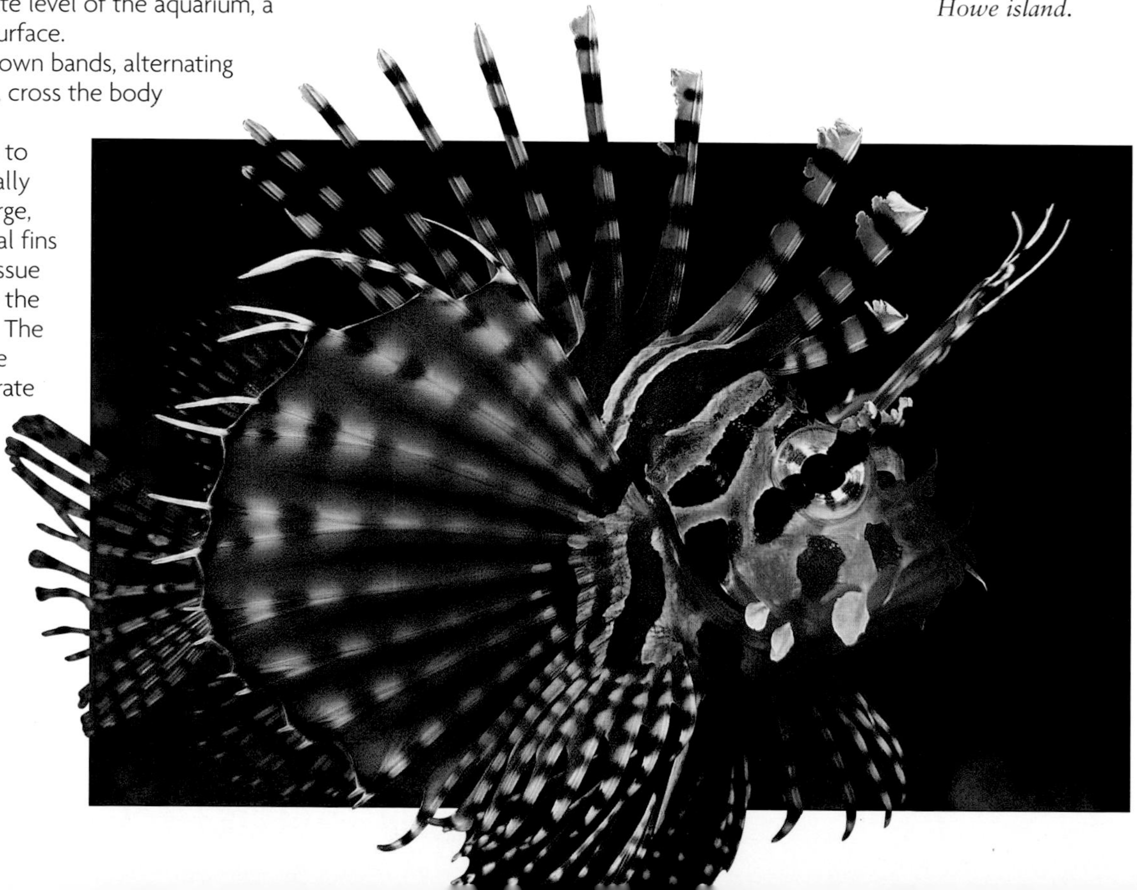

▶ Origins

From South Africa to Samoa, south Japan to Lord Howe island.

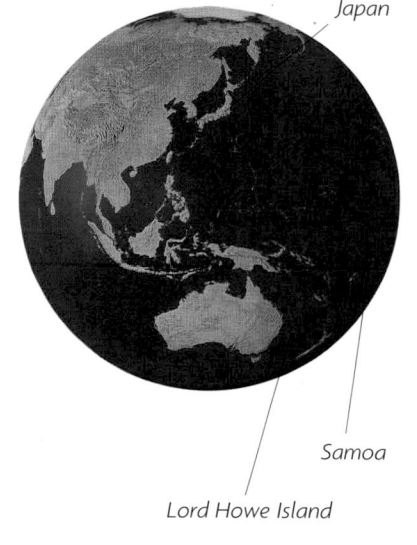

Japan

Samoa

Lord Howe Island

▶ *Fishkeeping data*

Number per aquarium: One.
Community/species tank: Species.
Swimming area: Middle and lower levels.
Food: A wide appetite for all foods, especially 'meaty' derivatives.
Compatibility: Predatory with small fishes and some invertebrates.
Availability: Often available (wild-caught).
Captive breeding: No information.

LIONFISH or TURKEYFISH ● *Pterois volitans*

FAMILY: SCORPAENIDAE (LIONFISHES)

Unlike the previous species, which is classed as a dwarf lionfish by fishkeepers, this is the real thing and quite fantastic in all its enlarged beauty.

Once again, the reddish brown-striped body is surrounded by a huge 'plumage' of fins. Although separated, each one of the first dozen rays of the dorsal fin has a backing of membranous tissue, giving them the appearance of feathers. Similarly, the rays of the huge pectoral fins are separate, with decorated tissue along their length. The function of these large fins is to herd prey into a convenient area for feeding on, and it is not hard to imagine a number of lionfish acting collectively, using their fins as capes to round up their next meal.

This species, usually seen 'drifting with intent' around rock faces and under coral ledges in public aquariums, seems to spend more time off the seabed than its smaller relatives.

Origins

From Malaysia to Pitcairn Island, south Japan to Lord Howe Island.

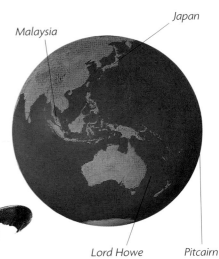

Japan

Malaysia

Lord Howe Island

Pitcairn Island

Fishkeeping data

Number per aquarium: One.
Community/species tank: Community (with large fish) or species tank.
Swimming area: All levels.
Food: All 'meaty' foods.
Compatibility: Predatory.
Availability: Regularly available (wild-caught).
Captive breeding: No information.

FAMILY: MONOCANTHIDAE (FILEFISHES)

It is hard to describe the characteristics of a species that frequents floating seaweeds and models itself accordingly. The body shape, once determined, is greyish white with a few brown blotches on the lower flanks and a couple of dark spots higher up. Its outline and actual surface is further disguised by a covering of tassel-like appendages, and a number of thin brown lines also cross the body in a branchlike network. The fins are mostly clear with a little speckling, and the caudal fin is attached to the body by a very short and narrow caudal peduncle. The pelvic fins are but a single spine. The tiny snout is beaklike, ideal for browsing and grazing on algae and polyp growths.

Once acclimatised to aquarium foods, this fish is a popular favourite. Fortunately, it is unlikely to attain its full natural size in the home aquarium.

The tassel-like appendages disguise the fish's presence amongst seaweeds.

▶ Origins

Waters around Malaysia, south Japan and the Great Barrier Reef.

Japan

Malaysia

Great Barrier Reef

▶ Fishkeeping data

Number per aquarium: One.
Community/species tank: Community.
Swimming area: Middle and lower levels.
Food: Most foods (including vegetable matter and meaty foods) once acclimatised. If necessary, offer live foods at first.
Compatibility: Fairly peaceful, but may nibble enquiringly at other fish without causing physical damage – only annoyance.
Availability: Often available (wild-caught).
Captive breeding: No information.

The widely spread caudal fin is attached to the body by a very slender, fragile-looking caudal peduncle.

YELLOW-FACED JAWFISH ● *Opisthognathus aurifrons*

FAMILY: OPISTHOGNATHIDAE (JAWFISHES)

For a good look at this species you will need to be patient until it is confident enough to emerge fully from its burrow. Then you can see that the long, cylindrical body is a most delicate blue, with a bright yellow, blunt head. The dorsal fin runs almost the complete length of the body and is mirrored by the anal fin, which occupies two-thirds of the ventral length. The pectoral fins are yellow, the pelvic and caudal fins blue. The dark eye is very large and the mouth, terminally situated at the tip of the blunt snout, is ideally placed for shifting grains of substrate material during excavation of the burrow.

Sex differentiation is difficult, but should breeding occur, then it is reported that the male takes on the incubating duties of this mouthbrooding species.

Fishkeeping data

Number per aquarium: One (possibly more in a species tank).
Community/species tank: Community or species tank.
Swimming area: Lower levels.
Food: Meaty foods. It is a good idea to mince these up and distribute them near to the fish's burrow.
Compatibility: Peaceful and shy.
Availability: Regularly available (wild-caught).
Captive breeding: No information.

▶ Origins

Opisthognathus *contains several species other than this one and all are found in waters ranging from Florida and the Bahamas to Barbados and Venezuela.*

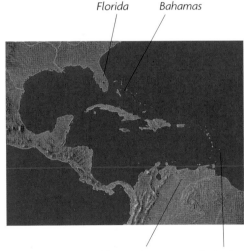

Florida   Bahamas

Venezuela   Barbados

The rear blue portion of the fish's body is usually hidden from view as it sits vertically in its burrow.

FAMILY: CALLIONYMIDAE (DRAGONETS)

Being blunt-headed, flat-bottomed and almost cylindrical, the body shape of this fish is very similar to that of the better-known bottom-dwelling species, such as blennies and gobies. There are two dorsal fins, the first of which is usually carried like a banner.

The basic body colour is light green, but this is overlaid with patches of dark green ringed with gold, black and blue. These blotches also appear in the dorsal, anal and pelvic fins, while the caudal and pectoral fins are a plain yellowish green. The high-set eye has a gold and black rim.

Males are generally equipped with brighter colours and extensions to the dorsal and anal fins. There is some belief that any highly coloured species (fish or invertebrates) are necessarily poisonous and advertise this fact accordingly; whether this toxicity risk actually applies to the mucus of this species is subject to conjecture.

The bizarre patterning of the psychedelic fish makes it difficult to spot on the substrate.

Origins

From the Philippines, throughout Indonesia and northwestern Australia.

Indonesia

Northwestern Australia

Philippines

Fishkeeping data

Number per aquarium: One or two.
Community/species tank: Suitably stocked community aquarium, but a species tank is probably better.
Swimming area: Lower level.
Food: Requires copious amounts of live foods.
Compatibility: Shy, but constantly on the lookout for food.
Availability: Often available (wild-caught).
Captive breeding: No information.

FAMILY: CALLIONYMIDAE (DRAGONETS)

The scaleless body of this fish is covered with an amazing tangle of contrasting colours that obviously reminded the original describer of the brilliantly coloured robes worn by ancient Chinese dignitaries. Golds, reds and greens are all intertwined across the body; nor are the fins excluded from this rainbow effect, having purple edges in addition to those colours spreading from the body. The caudal fin has gold lines radiating from the caudal peduncle and the large pelvic fins are decorated with purple/green spots. The first ray of the first dorsal fin is projected and carried stiffly like a flag.

Breeding

From very limited reports of aquarium breeding, it seems that internal fertilisation of eggs occurs before their release as floating eggs into open water. While this may be true, there are no reports of any viable fry being raised to maturity.

▶ Origins

Waters around the Philippines and Java, from the Ryukyu Islands south of Japan to the Great Barrier Reef.

Philippines

Ryukyu Islands

Japan

Java

Great Barrier Reef

▶ Fishkeeping data

Number per aquarium: One or two.
Community/species tank: Suitably stocked community aquarium, but a species tank is probably better.
Swimming area: Lower level.
Food: Requires copious amounts of live foods.
Compatibility: Shy, but constantly on the lookout for food.
Availability: Often available (wild-caught).
Captive breeding: Has spawned in captivity, but not a regular occurrence and no reports of surviving fry are known.

INDEX

Page numbers in **bold** indicate major entries; *italics* refer to captions and annotations; plain type indicates other text entries.

CREDITS

The majority of the images in this book have been supplied by Max Gibbs of Photomax. The publishers would also like to thank the following photographers for providing images, credited here by page number and position: B(Bottom), T(Top), C(Centre), BL(Bottom Left), etc.

Bruce Coleman Collection: 8(Franco Banfi), 42(Charles & Sandra Hood), 64(Charles & Sandra Hood), 75(Jane Burton) ● Frank Lane Picture Agency: 38 ● Kim Osborn: 16 ● Geoffrey Rogers © Interpet Publishing: 6

Illustrations by Phil Holmes and Stuart Watkinson © Interpet Publishing. The maps have been produced using Terra Forma files created by Andromeda Interactive Ltd, Abingdon, Oxfordshire.

The publishers would like to thank Maidenhead Aquatics Ascot Waterworld, Country Gardens Garden Centre, Windlesham, Surrey for providing facilities for practical photography.

The information and recommendations in this book are given without any guarantees on the part of the author and publisher, who disclaim any liability with the use of this material.